THANKS TO MY PARENTS BUZZIE AND
JAY. YOU NEVER STOPPED LOVING ME NO
MATTER WHAT.

STOP THINKING THOUGHTS THAT SCARE YOU

A SELF HELP GUIDE OF PRACTICAL
TOOLS TO ELIMINATE FEAR AND ANXIETY
AND LIVE A LIFE OF ABUNDANCE

NOA SHAW

FOR MORE VISIT WWW.NOASHAW.COM

OR EMAIL NOASHAW@MAC.COM

TWENTY SIX PUBLISHING

INTRODUCTION

It shouldn't need to be so fucking hard, this life on earth. It's just life on earth. It doesn't need to be the end of you or me. This is life on earth. It's just life on earth.

--Snow Patrol, Life on Earth

I should be dead.

I've had people try to kill me many times. I've been shot at, with bullets just barely grazing my ear. I've been stabbed in the stomach and have a long scar to show for it. I've had a couple of guys try to throw me off the roof of a fucking building. I've tried to kill myself numerous times. I've even walked away from a car wreck that no one else survived.

But I'm still here.

I had my first near-death experience when I was about four years old. I was living with my parents in suburban New Jersey. I was in the front yard playing in the snow, and my parents were watching me from the porch. Suddenly, a snow-plow lost control and began barreling down the hill straight towards where I was standing. I froze. While this event was just a matter of seconds, I have a distinct memory of seeing terror flash in my parents' eyes as they were watching this happen and then shifting to see the horror in the snowplow driver's eyes. And even though I understood that death was imminent, I was calm.

The driver was able to stop the blade of the snowplow about a foot from my body. He would have easily sliced me in half, and I would have been dead, buried in a pile of snow. Thankfully he was able to shift the gear to stop the machine just in time.

Since this early incident, I have always been perfectly calm in the face of death. Is that a good or bad thing? I'm not sure. But I am sure that the fearlessness I experienced has contributed to my attraction to danger and conscious disregard for my own life over the years.

And it's not really any wonder that I gravitated towards danger and recklessness. I spent a good 40 years of my life as a miserable person living in a constant state of self-loathing and emotional turmoil. As a result, I lied, cheated, stole, took advantage of people, and did some truly terrible things to others and myself.

But after years of destruction, I found a better way to live.

After walking through hell and surviving, I have turned away from the darkness and created a life filled with love and light. While I'm not living a life of celebrity or riches, I am living in a world that's rich in love and joy, and I've dedicated myself to helping shepherd others on their path towards a brighter, more fulfilling existence.

Years ago, I was a walking shell of a human being. I had nothing. I had no money, barely any clothing, and I was lost. I was so broken in every single way possible. Yet, as I sit here now and write this, I'm in my comfortable apartment in Brooklyn, NY. I have a wonderful job teaching physical fitness to hundreds of people each week, which allows me to inspire and help people through challenges. I have a life coaching business that allows me to guide clients towards achieving their goals. I have a loving and compassionate family that accepts me for who I am despite the pain that I put them through over the years. I have a group of kind and supportive friends. And I have more food and clothing than I need.

In this book, I share with you some of the tools that I've developed along my journey to help manage my demons and live in peace. This book serves as a guide to help you become a better person, shift your perspective, and overcome some of the obstacles that you might face along the way. I am not sharing these tools with you from a place of expert authority, and these tools are not a substitute for therapy with a doctor or qualified therapist. These are merely techniques that have worked for me and others I've coached, and I want to share them here in case they might be of service to you.

In the coming pages, I will teach you how to silence the inner self-critic—that voice in your head that says: *I'm not good enough. I'm scared. I'm lonely. I'm sad. I'm depressed. I'm unstable. I'm unworthy.* All those negative thoughts that rattle around our brains and create a false sense of paralysis; that feeling of being hopelessly **stuck.**

I know that feeling. I've lived with that feeling for much of my life. But I came through the other side. Let me show you how.

Music has always played an integral role in my life. My maternal grandmother was an accomplished classical pianist and studied with Van Cliburn. To this day, I can still hear the sound of her playing and picture her tiny, strong hands flying expertly across the keyboard. Her musicality inspired my own passion for music, which continues to this day. Even in my darkest times, there was always an artist who perfectly captured the same emotions I was feeling through the poetry of their lyrics and musical score.

Today, I get to play music for a living in my fitness classes, and I use it to curate an emotional experience and connect with my riders on a spiritual level. To pay homage to the influence of music on my life, I quote certain lyrics throughout this book that reflect my experiences, feelings, and certain of my lessons.

I hope you find this resource useful. If I can help even one person overcome their pain, then everything I went through in my own life was well worth it.

TABLE OF CONTENTS

CHAPTER ONE

I FELL OFF

Standing on a hill in the mountain of dreams, telling
myself it's not as hard, hard as it seems.

--Led Zeppelin, Going to California

As I sit here today with my beautiful life, the love I experience, the family and friends that surround me, the fulfilling job I have, my message is clear:

YOU CAN DO THIS.

If I can do this, anyone can.

I came from a great family. A wonderful, loving, kind family.

I am a White man, and as a result, I've had a lot of privileges. My family was middle income when I was younger, but by the time I was in my teens, my father had climbed the corporate ladder, and we were very comfortably upper income. I had every asset available for me to succeed.

As a kid, I was tested with a genius-level IQ, and by the time I graduated high school, I was in the bottom 5 percent of my graduating class. I had a near-perfect score on my SATs (which I took drunk and high), but I barely ever attended class and had no real interest in going to college.

Intelligence means nothing if your feelings and actions are not positively aligned. And, for me, my self-hatred and destructive behavior negatively guided my life for so many years that being smart hardly mattered. If there was a right way of doing things, I did the exact opposite. And that brought me to some really dark places in my life.

I had the best parents ever——the kind of parents that people dream of having. When I was in high school, other kids would always ask, "Hey, can I stay at your house? My parents are fighting; they're going through a divorce." My parents adored each other, and that love just radiated around them. My friends viewed my house as a sort of sanctuary because my parents were so warm and welcoming and kind. When I was younger, I took advantage of that kindness. I could be very charming, very earnest, and I was very persuasive. I manipulated them into trusting me, and I took advantage of their kindness and did some truly terrible things.

In my early years, we constantly moved due to the nature of my father's job. He was fiercely dedicated to building his career in publishing, but as a result, I ended up going to nine schools in three different states over the course of 12 years. Because we moved around so much, I was always the new kid, and I was always trying to fit in.

As it was, I felt inherently different from everyone around me. For starters, I had the name 'Noah,' which in the 1970s was a pretty unusual name. Kids would taunt me by calling me 'Noah's Ark,' which I just hated. (I later dropped the 'h' and officially changed my name to 'Noa,' which in Hawaiian means 'freedom,' and is how people wrote it when I lived in Maui, which I discuss later in this book.)

We were a Jewish family that ultimately landed in the mostly Irish Catholic suburbs of Fairfield County, Connecticut. My mother had been raised by very intellectual parents who read voraciously and studied science, political theory, music, and even Sanskrit. They read Marx and believed in the ideological tenets of communism and socialism, and they were also strict atheists. As a result, I had no sense of religion—cultural or spiritual—with the exception of family gatherings on Christmas and Easter because those felt like American holidays rather than religious ones. We never went to the temple, and we never observed any of the Jewish holidays. As a result, I never identified with or belonged to any cultural community.

I didn't look like the other kids in Fairfield County. They were mostly blonde with blue eyes, perfectly sloping noses, and barely any body hair. I had this crazy mop of curly dark hair and bad teeth. I went to orthodontists to fix my teeth, but because I had a speech impediment, my tongue would hit my teeth in a certain way such that even after years of braces, they went right back to being crooked, angular, and weird. I still don't like my teeth, but at this point, they are what they are.

By the time I was 13, I had a full coat of body hair everywhere—my arms, my legs, my chest, my back. I was by far the hairiest person I knew, and other kids would mock me because of it. Whenever I had my shirt off, whether at the beach or in the locker room, kids would joke about my 'sweater vest' of body hair.

So, being this new kid and feeling very different, very alone and isolated, drove me to develop a series of unhealthy coping mechanisms from a very early age.

When I was finally able to walk to elementary school by myself, I would stop at the candy store before school. Candy wasn't that expensive back then and, with whatever couple of dollars I had, I'd buy as much candy as I could. I would arrive at school with this big bag of candy and start handing it out to everyone, and they loved it. My classmates were excited to see me and would flock around me. I realized this was a great way to ingratiate myself with the other kids. This was a way to stop feeling ostracized. I was trading candy for acceptance and friendship.

As I grew older, I continued to use this strategy in different and more nefarious contexts. At one point, in middle school, I came up with a scam to trick people into giving me money because I realized that I could turn my strategy into a money-making scheme—killing two birds with one stone, so to speak.

In the mid-1970s, the band Kiss was one of the biggest bands in the world, and they were coming to Harford, Connecticut, close to where I lived. I was sort of 'connected,' in that my father ran the local newspaper there, so I told everyone at school that I was going to be backstage at the concert and would get autographs for whoever wanted one in exchange for $1 each.

"Oh my god, that's so cool!" the kids said, eyes wide.

A bunch of them submitted orders for autographs.

So, on the night of the concert, I went home after school and spent the night in my room copying the signatures of the band members off one of Kiss's album covers. I signed a ton of pictures myself. I never went to the concert.

The next day at school, I sold all of the forged autographs.

"Yeah, the concert was mind-blowing!" I said.

It was all a complete lie. But now everyone loved me and thought I was so cool, and I made some money out of it too.

Whenever I found myself in a new environment, I would offer people something to help me get past my insecurity about how they perceived me and manipulate them into liking me. It always worked. And later on, I replaced candy and counterfeit autographs with weed, coke, acid, and ecstasy.

My descent into drugs and alcohol was not terribly surprising, given that I had wanted to escape myself for as long as I can remember. I had my first drink at age 10. My dad had a liquor cabinet in the house, and I swiped a bottle of Wild Turkey from the cabinet, headed out to the woods behind my house, and started to drink. And even though I made myself horribly sick, the drinking somehow also felt really good. So, I drank some more.

I smoked my first joint about a year later, at age 11. I had a friend who had an older sister—probably 13 or 14 years old—selling weed in our little neighborhood. She told me to go up the block and deliver this dime bag of weed to one of the neighbors and collect money from them as payment. So, I did what she said, and I handed the guy the weed and collected the money. In exchange, she gave me a joint to smoke. But what I realized I really liked, in addition to the weed, was the adrenaline rush from doing this little transaction. I liked making the deal, and I liked collecting the money. This was the prelude to many, much larger, drug deals in the future.

When I was 16 years old, I would drive to school every day with my best friend, Rusty. Rusty had a head of wild red hair; thus, the name. His dad was a top marketing executive at Ogilvy & Mather and represented Schmidt Brewing Company, so he had like a hundred cases of beer lying around his house. Rusty would wear this long dark trench coat and stuff cans of beer into the inside pockets. It was beers for everyone all day, every day. We were a match made in heaven. Eventually, our mutual affinity for drinking turned into a partnership of reckless adventure and crime. Together, we probably broke into dozens of homes in our small Connecticut enclave, stealing thousands of dollars worth of items to pawn to help fund our drinking and drug habits.

Rusty and I would always stop by the liquor store on our way to school, and there was an old shopkeeper named Charlie who managed the store and would sell us whatever bottles we wanted. Charlie was an alcoholic with a big old gin rummy nose. He lived in the back of the store and just drank his life away. Rusty and I would buy a quart of orange juice and empty some of the juice to make room for the pint of vodka we brought from Charlie. I can't think of a single morning that we just drank the carton of orange juice without pouring vodka into it.

One morning, as we were speeding down the highway,

drinking our screwdrivers at 7 am, I had an uncomfortable revelation. I looked over at Rusty in the passenger seat and said, "You know what? I'm an alcoholic."

He just looked back at me, smiled, and said, "Yeah, man. I am too."

I wasn't proud in that moment, but I was resigned. I really believed that this was who I was and all I'd ever be. I was only 16, and I already saw that there was simply no viable future for me in this world outside of my addiction.

This feeling of hopelessness was a recurring theme as I got older. For years, I would sit alone in my room and have the same self-defeating thoughts about myself. I'd think with resignation of the destruction I was causing as I was causing it. I'd think about the opportunities that I squandered and the loneliness that I felt. And in response to those thoughts, I'd think: *Well, this is just the hand I was dealt. This is my lot in life. This is just who I am, and I have to accept that. I'm never going to have a beautiful life.*

Rusty died some years later from his alcoholism and drug addiction. He was alone in his apartment in Chicago watching tv and doing lines of coke when his heart just gave out. Ironically, I found myself in Chicago trying to commit suicide a few years before that, but instead of dying, I wound up in a rehab facility, which started my long road to recovery. There's something oddly symbiotic about the fact that I found my sobriety in the same city where Rusty died.

My alcoholism eventually grew into a formidable drug addiction as well. And while I was able to consume copious amounts of alcohol and smoke a ton of weed, I was a real heavyweight champion when it came to snorting endless piles of cocaine.

At one point, in my early 20s, I had snorted so much cocaine that I developed a permanently stuffy nose. My nasal passages were so blocked that not only did I have trouble breathing but—more importantly to me at the time—I had trouble getting the cocaine up my nostrils. Nothing was working, not even straws. I had developed this crazy mass in the middle of my septum that was blocking everything up.

So, this one time I was on a plane on my way to stay with friends in Utah. At that time, in the mid-1980s, it was easy to carry bags of coke on the plane. There were no security checkpoints. No one was checking your luggage. So, I was sitting there on this flight, drinking so heavily that my entire body was shaking. I got up to go to the bathroom with this bag of coke, and I don't know if it was the turbulence or if it was me, but I ended up spilling the bag all over the bathroom sink and floor. Panicked, I wiped my hands all over the floor and the counter to gather the coke and just shoveled it all in my mouth. I couldn't snort it anyway since I couldn't get anything up my damn nose.

When I landed, I went straight to my friends' house in Salt Lake City. They both worked in a local hospital and had all of these medical instruments in the bathroom. I still couldn't figure out what was blocking my nose. I kept trying to get up there to figure it out, but I couldn't quite reach the mass. So, I grabbed a pair of forceps out of their medicine cabinet, shoved them up my nose, and yanked out this fucking rock of crust and blood, leaving a huge hole in the middle of my nasal passage. I still have that hole in my nose to this day.

The fact that I pulled out the middle of my nose didn't even register. I was way more excited that I could finally snort lines again! I ran straight to my supply of coke.

"This is awesome!"

The physical destruction that I inflicted on my body over the years was impressive. Aside from my nose, I had damaged my liver and my heart. I picked up smoking by the time I was 11, so my lungs were shot. I was bald by the time I was in my 20s, which I'm convinced was due to the constate state of stress and anxiety I lived in. At one point, I lived with a scaly red rash all over my body—head to toe—that was caused by the stress and agitation of doing so much coke.

For years, I had a cough that persisted all day, every day. I would wake up in the morning thinking it was finally gone, and then I'd suddenly feel that little tickle rise in the back of my throat. I'd cough and cough and cough every second of the damn day. I got tested for AIDS, cancer, everything you can imagine, and every test came back negative. The doctors finally diagnosed it as a nervous disorder, which I've ultimately learned to control by using some of the techniques I describe in this book.

The physical damage was only a manifestation of the emotional pain. The persistent judging of myself as a loser, unlovable, not worthy of life; the constant destruction of my self-worth; and my inability to love myself or anyone else for that matter, all led me back to feeling more stuck and engaging in more destructive behavior. It was like I was trapped in this futile cycle of emotional pain leading to physical pain leading to more emotional pain, and nothing was ever going to change.

The darkest place I've ever been was when I was sitting on the edge of my bed, pressing a gun to my own head. I've tried to kill myself 3 times. It took a long time for me to go from the child slinging candy in grade school to a man ready to end his own life. The descent didn't happen all at once. It actually took years to erode my sense of well-being until I hit rock bottom. But the feelings and the downward spiral started very early on and only snowballed as I got older and had access to more dangerous substances and exposure to more harrowing situations.

In my mid-late teens, I would take the train into New York City at night to party at bars and nightclubs. In the late 1970s/early 1980s, Studio 54 was the place to be and be seen, and all the celebrities—anyone you'd want to rub elbows with from Andy Warhol to Mick Jagger to John Lennon to Brooke Shields—were partying there. And, of course, cocaine was like the biggest thing back then. They even had this huge moon and coke spoon hanging by the DJ booth—the spoon was feeding coke into the moon's nose. And I showed up with enough blow for everyone.

On this one particular occasion, a bit later—probably in my early 20s—I had been up all night partying. It was 7 am on a Sunday. I was sitting in my car, parked on a Manhattan side street, cranking music and snorting coke as the sun was rising. As day broke and the city started to come alive, people began emerging from their apartment buildings to run errands, get coffee, pick up the paper, and so on.

I watched a family come out of their building—a couple with two kids—laughing, holding hands, and just savoring the start of the day. Another couple walked out of a brownstone, arm-in-arm. Everyone on the street just seemed so damn happy, living in this bright shiny light. And there I was, in my shitty little car, alone with a pile of cocaine in my lap and nowhere to go and no one to be with. I was the same outsider I'd always been. I so clearly remember this moment, and I so clearly remember thinking I would never have that life. I would never be happy. I would never know that kind of joy, that human connection, that contact, that deep sense of belonging. I would never be the guy holding his girlfriend's hand and feeling loved. It was almost as if I was living in black and white while the rest of the world was living in color.

That moment was so profound that I can still remember it today with such clarity. And everything I do, every single thing I do now, is motivated by my desire to never be back there again, to never be that guy on the side of the road thinking, *I'm not worthy of a good life.* Because I am. No matter what has happened to me or what I've done in my past. I am so worthy of a good life, and so are you.

I'm sharing all of this with you merely to give you some insight into how my story evolved, and the genesis of my pain, and the coping mechanisms that started me on what became a severely destructive path. I want you to understand that no matter who you are in this world—rich, poor, young, old, male, female, or other—we all have the capacity to feel intense self-loathing and pain and, as a result, become self-destructive. I want to assure you that there is a better way to live.

It's not that there's a divine antidote for the insecurity and degrading thoughts I had about myself—I still to this day struggle with looking at myself in the mirror—but there are strategies I've used to stop being so unkind to myself. Blocking the noise in my head and speaking to myself more kindly has been a key element of my growth.

I come from the worst situations. I've dealt with, life coached, and worked with people who have been through the most harrowing and traumatic experiences. Because of my life experiences over more than a decade of helping other people, I know I can pass on to you some important skills that can help you change your life for the better.

I'm a fairly peaceful and loving person now. When I tell people stories about myself in the past and how I was, the people who know me today have a hard time reconciling that person with who I am now. They have a hard time understanding how I could go from being someone in so much pain and turmoil to being someone so kind and loving and serene. It just doesn't seem right to them.

There are a handful of people who knew me back when I was in that pain. When they see me now, they say, "God damn, dude, I can't even believe you're the same person."

When I was three years sober, I ran into an old college friend while sitting in a deli in New York City. I was sitting at a table, and this guy approached me and asked, "Are you Noa Shaw?"

"Yep."

"Man, I went to college with you for a year," he said.

This was 6 or 7 years after I left college (I dropped out after freshman year).

"We all thought you were dead," he continued. "We heard a rumor that you either died of a drug overdose or in a car accident—no one knew which one, and we could never get the story straight. Everyone had different versions of what had happened. We even held a vigil for you. Like a bunch of us got together at a bar and talked about you and the good memories we had. I can't believe you're sitting right here!"

In my high school yearbook, I was voted, 'Most likely to go to prison.' That was how little the students in my school thought of me. It wasn't that they didn't think I was a good person; they just thought that there was no way I could sustain the crazy and destructive life I was living.

But here I am—alive and well and about to turn 57 years old as I write this. And while it wasn't easy getting here—in fact, it was really fucking hard—I've managed to pull through, and I couldn't be more grateful every single day for this gift of my life.

So, now I'm a healer, helper, guide, teacher, life coach. I'm a speaker. I try to motivate people to become the best version of themselves. I teach guided meditations to help center people and silence the negative chatter in their brains. I am now precisely the opposite of the person I was in all of these stories I've shared. The reward on the other side of the darkness, on the other side of the hard work, is incredible.

I always say, the opposite of fear is love. There's no shortage of either in this world, and you get to choose which one you want to draw upon every day. I know it's easier said than done, but you need to do the work to train your brain to allow yourself to tap into the love and silence the fear. It's only when you're existing in that space that you can truly be serene and be open to living in truth.

That's why I always tell people to **STOP THINKING THOUGHTS THAT SCARE YOU.** If you live in persistent thoughts that are fear-driven—the *I'm not good enough*; the *what-if*; the *worst-case scenario for the future*; the *past regrets*—you're living in moments that are not real but are merely projections of your fear onto various circumstances and situations. That unhealthy thought process can be released, and you can walk free. That's the goal we're shooting for.

Sounds aspirational, I know. But you can get there. If we're going to get you to a new place, you need a roadmap and a set of clear steps. Again, the tools I'm about to share with you aren't cure-alls or a replacement for therapy. They're just useful skills to develop and implement in your daily life to help refocus your brain and silence the destabilizing voice of fear.

Picking up this book is the start of your journey, and in the following chapters, I will lead you through some practices that you can use to help you live a more beautiful life.

CHAPTER 2

AN ATTITUDE OF GRATITUDE

∽

The channel's changing, the heart is racing, from voices on the wire. The soul is yearning, the coal is burning, the ember starts a fire.

--Foo Fighters, I Am A River

Why gratitude? Gratitude is an essential building block when laying the foundation for the life you want to build. I'm not going to tell you how to live your life, but I'm going to try to help you live it well. A fundamental part of living well is to live with a grateful heart.

> Gratitude allows us to let go of our fear-based thinking by demanding that we focus on positivity and love. In doing so, gratitude helps us extinguish mental pain. I often say that you cannot be angry with a grateful heart. And it's really true—when we're focused on what we have and the beauty in our lives, we show our love and our best selves to the world. #TheMoreYouNoa

I'm going to introduce you to a cast of characters throughout this book who were my mentors and healers at various points in my journey. Each taught me an important lesson that has helped me live a better life.

The first mentor I want you to meet is a man named Kalua.

I moved to Hawaii in 1991, a few years after I got sober. I was 28 years old. I had been living back at my parents' house after dropping out of college, living in many states across the country, and doing about 10 or 12 stints in various rehab facilities. One night I was lying in bed watching tv, and I saw a tourism commercial for Maui—the beautiful volcanos rising above the Pacific Ocean, the rugged coastline, the palm trees, the waterfalls. It was incredibly beautiful and enticing, and so the next day, I bought a one-way ticket to Maui. No money. No job. I just went.

Kalua was one of the first people I met on the island. He was this tiny, skinny Hawaiian dude with some worn-out tattoos and a super chill, warm smile. He was a friend of a friend, and when I was introduced to him, we clicked right away.

Even though I was sober when I met Kalua, I was still depressed and generally unhappy with my life. I had gotten divorced a few years prior (which I get into later in this book), and I was generally feeling pretty lonely and without purpose. Kalua and I had a long talk about the laundry list of things I felt were wrong with me. He listened silently, and after my venting session, he looked at me calmly and said, "Noa, you need to shift your thinking towards an attitude of gratitude."

Now, at this point, I had been regularly attending Alcoholics Anonymous meetings, and in almost every meeting room,

I'd see a sign saying, 'Have an Attitude of Gratitude.' They had always seemed like just words to me. *What did that even really mean? Is it just some bullshit saying to make people feel better about themselves?*

But it was not. After hearing this message delivered by Kalua—a man whom I greatly respected and adored—I decided to at least *try* to experiment with the practice of focusing on what I was grateful for rather than all of the things I thought were wrong with my life. And in time, everything shifted.

It didn't happen instantly. Living with an attitude of gratitude is like strength training—as you practice it, you're building a muscle that you hadn't had before, and that takes time. But I assure you if you just commit to this for one month, you will see significant changes in your life and overall well-being.

In fact, there are many scientific studies that prove the link between higher levels of gratitude and overall well-being. Studies show that gratitude mitigates stress and depression, leads to more fulfilling relationships, and increases overall life satisfaction. While scientists don't yet know how or why gratitude develops in the brain, the outcome of practicing gratitude is clearly positively impactful.

So how do you do this? I suggest you start by creating a ritual around gratitude. What is a ritual? It's a plan that you follow consistently. Be regimented about it and hold yourself accountable *to yourself.*

Your gratitude ritual can be the first thing you do in the morning. So, for example, most of us wake up and have some sort of beverage—whether it's a glass of water or a cup of coffee or tea. I personally love to drink iced coffee year-round. Iced coffee is God's gift to me to help me start my day. Whatever you drink, take a moment to focus on gratitude while you're sipping it. Put down your phone. Turn off your TV. Just sit and focus on a few things you're grateful for. Put a pen and a piece of paper next to the spot where you sip your morning drink every day. I have my coffee in bed, so I keep my pen and paper on my nightstand. Start off by simply writing down 3 things you're grateful for.

For me today, I wrote: *I love my parents. I'm grateful to be sober. I love my job.*

Just focus on forcing yourself to do this every day—just as you would brush your teeth. Put a note, timer, whatever you need to remind yourself, so you don't skip it. And if you do miss it, remember that this is a learning process—we're building a muscle—so don't judge yourself and simply go back to it the next day. There's no room in any of this for self-pity or anger. It takes a while to build a ritual. Be easy and gentle on yourself. Allow yourself to be a student.

After a while, you'll start to feel this ritual take hold. At this point, you may want to go a little deeper with your list. While a more thoughtful and extensive list may require more effort and introspection, the results of your effort will have a more powerful impact on your life.

This is an example of a deeper list: *I'm grateful for the opportunity that each day brings for me to grow and work on myself. I'm grateful to have a set of tools that help me be a better person. I'm grateful to my friends and family who never gave up on me.*

About two years ago, I read an article about this woman in England who kept seeing those gratitude signs everywhere:

You've got to have an attitude of gratitude. You have to be grateful. Like me, she was very skeptical of it. She was not into it. It seemed like bullshit to her.

This woman was a writer. To prove her hypothesis, she decided that an interesting experiment would be for her to spend an entire year focusing on gratitude to the best of her ability. Now, before she decided to do this, she went to the doctor for a checkup, and the doctor performed a full workup on her. He checked her blood pressure, her heart, ran a full panel of blood tests—the whole nine yards. This woman was in her 50s, and the test results were as you'd expect them to be for someone her age who didn't particularly eat well or exercise.

Following that appointment, she started down her grateful path. She did gratitude journals, attended workshops on gratitude, and read books. She focused on gratitude in every way she could, every day for a whole year. She did not change a single thing about her diet or exercise regimen. And at the end of that year, she wrote that she had never felt better in her life. She felt an overwhelming sense of ease. The tension had drained from her life. She had better relationships with her friends and family. Every single aspect of her life had positively improved.

When she went back to the doctor for her next annual checkup, she had all of the same tests run that had been performed the year before. The doctor was shocked by the results. He had never seen anything like it—across the board, every aspect of her health had materially improved. So not only was she healthier mentally and emotionally, she was healthier physically. All because of her intentional thinking and acting with gratitude.

The incredibly simple yet powerful tool of gratitude has profoundly impacted my recovery and life overall. It has been especially useful during the darkest or most challenging times. I try not to use the word *hard;* I prefer the word *challenging* because I believe it's less negative. If I tell you something is hard, it doesn't sound fun. If I tell you something is challenging, then it sounds like something you can engage with positively and try to fix or solve.

A critical aspect of my personal gratitude practice has been to remind myself that I am enough exactly as I am. **As I am, I am enough**. What does this mean?

By 2007, I was living in LA. I had lost my sobriety and was smoking weed again. As a result, I landed in a Jewish rehab called *Beit T'Shuvah* in Culver City.

We studied Judaism and the Torah, and this was ironically my introduction to my own religion. There were people of every faith in this rehab facility because it was spiritually oriented, linking the Old Testament to the AA Big Book and the 12 steps. It also happened to be a place where people who had committed drug crimes went in exchange for a reduced sentence, which was how I ended up there.

Every morning they would wake us up at some ungodly hour—like 5 am—to study the Torah. We studied Judaism in relation to addiction and pain, and we were taught how recovery relates to many of the parables in the bible.

We learned that when Moses parted the Red Sea, the Israelites followed him while others drowned. Those who followed him were set free. The point was, those of us who are in brutal pain (for example, those of us in sobriety), who seek help and follow the path towards recovery, will be set free. Those who do not seek help will struggle to survive.

After a group meeting one day, I took a walk with Rabbi Andy, one of my many teachers and gurus. Rabbi Andy was a clean-cut, younger dude, probably mid-30s. He had been a guitar player in a punk rock band in Dallas and was also a junkie before getting sober, finding spirituality, and becoming a rabbi. I was lamenting everything that I had lost before I ended up in this rehab—15 years of sobriety, my business, a bunch of cash, my friends. He just nodded sympathetically and then turned to me and said, "You know Noa, **happy is the man who is happy with what he has**."

"What do you mean by that?" I asked.

"If you can be happy with exactly what you have in this life and feel that everything is good exactly as it is, you will feel a great sense of freedom. That perspective displaces the feeling of never having enough or never being enough." He added, "You must accept that you're perfect just as you are."

After this conversation with him, I decided to implement this affirmation into my daily life. I would simply regularly remind myself, "As I am, I am enough." This doesn't mean that we can't change things and shouldn't strive to grow. It just means that we start our growth from a place of acceptance and love.

You must remember that you were born a perfect creature of the universe. You were born loving and kind. The only thing that has changed about that state of being is your feelings and projections onto yourself and the world that surrounds you. You were not born angry. You were not born fearful. You were not born with hatred in your heart for anyone, including yourself. These are all learned feelings and behaviors that we must try to unlearn to become more at ease.

So how are we going to learn to slowly love ourselves? Take little acts of self-care every single day. Here are some suggestions:

Do Things for Others

I talk about this in more depth later in this book. When you're focusing on doing things for other people, you're not focused on yourself. When have you ever regretted volunteering at a food pantry or a toy drive or raising money for any other cause you believe in? Never. When we give ourselves to helping others, when we bring joy to the lives of others, we get out of our own way and help ourselves.

Doing for other people doesn't need to be charitable either. Buy your friend a coffee. Give your waitress a little extra tip. If you see a little something in a store that you think your friend will like, buy it for them. If I'm scrolling through Instagram and see an ad for a t-shirt that reminds me of one of my friends, I'll just order it for them. These little acts of kindness pay big dividends.

Do Things for Yourself.

While doing for others is of critical importance to our overall sense of well-being, so is doing things to care for yourself. It doesn't have to be anything big. Just think about the little indulgences that make you happy and shower yourself with some love.

For example, flowers are so healing and brighten up any space. So today, I want you to go out and get yourself a bouquet of flowers. If you don't like flowers, then get a plant. Put it in your home somewhere you spend a lot of time so you can look at it regularly. This should mark the beginning of you celebrating your own life; you loving on yourself. When the flowers die (or you kill the plant—like I sometimes do), then go out and get yourself another one to remind yourself of the journey you're on and the beauty that you deserve every single day.

Other acts of self-love and self-care that you can take include caring for your body. Your body is the only constant home you'll ever have. Discipline yourself to exercise; take a class; do some yoga; go for a hike or even a walk to the park; let the sun shine on your face. Eat something healthy—not because you don't like the shape of your body or because want to lose weight—but because you want to *feel good*. Get a manicure. Get a massage. Again, self-love and self-care don't have to cost a lot of money and don't have to be hugely indulgent. It's the consistent practice of treating yourself to little things that make you happy and set you at ease—that is key.

Forgive Yourself

I want you to treat yourself like you would treat a puppy or a child. You would be gentle and loving with that puppy. It would make mistakes, and your response would be, "Oh, puppy, you peed on the rug, and you chewed up that shoe." But you wouldn't harm the puppy. You wouldn't give it away. You'd simply clean up the pee and forgive the puppy. The same thing with a child. If a child makes a mistake, would you harm the child? Would you badger them and call them terrible names? Of course not. You'd love them and teach them how to do things better. Do the same for yourself. Your mistakes don't make you any less worthy of love and care and forgiveness.

You Are Worthy

I want you to buy some post-it notes. Think of some positive words to describe yourself.

Now, I want you to put these post-it notes with these words all over your apartment or house—on your refrigerator, by your desk, on your computer screen, next to your bed, on your bathroom mirror, everywhere.

The phrases on these post-it notes should say things like:

I love myself.

I am beautiful.

I am worthy of love.

As I am, I am enough.

I get to do this job.

To carry this work forward, I want you to take this practice a little deeper. Take a piece of paper and draw a vertical line down the center. I want you to title the left column 'I am not,' and in this column, I want you to write down all of the ways in which you think you are lacking.

I am unworthy. I am a terrible person. I am not loving. I am ugly. I am scared. I am desperate. I am stuck. I am invisible.

When you're done, I want you to stop and look at the list. Then I want you to title the right column 'I am,' and in this column, I want you to write down the antonym for each adjective you put to describe yourself in the column on the left.

I am unworthy becomes *I am worthy. I am scared* becomes *I am courageous.*

This exercise forces you to look at your fears and address

them with love. Because really, you are the exact opposite of everything that you fear you are. That is your truth—fear is never the truth. Fear, anger, and lonely thoughts are how we feel about ourselves and the circumstances we're in, but that doesn't make them real. Understand that.

Now, one final exercise. I challenge you to do this—it may be a little uncomfortable, but it's worth it. I want you to find three friends or family members, and I want you to ask each of them to describe you in three words. Just do it. Make a list on your phone of what they all say. When you look at those 9 things on your list, I assure you they will look completely different than the list you created on your own. See that new list. Believe that new list. Internalize that new list. It's the people who love us—the people who see us without the filter of the noise in our brains—who see us as we really are. That's the truth.

CHAPTER THREE

THE TIME IS NOW

∽

*Right now, catch a magic moment, do it, right here
and now, it means everything.*

--Van Halen, Right Now

The only real time is right now.

I've spent a lot of time in my life thinking and dreaming in fear. For many years, I lived in fear of the unknown. I always feared what might happen next. *Oh my god, something terrible is going to happen.* Or I spent a lot of time lamenting the past and looking back with regret and disgust at myself for all of my failures. *Oh my god, what the fuck have I done to my life?*

In fact, everything I had done in the past had created a narrative in my mind where I could only imagine a horrible future ahead. There was never a good outcome in my thoughts. I felt like I was constantly wandering aimlessly in dark woods without knowing the way out. And when you can't find the way out, all you see in front of you is a hopelessly endless path that seemingly goes nowhere, and you're constantly anxious about what might lurk around the bend.

There was never a good outcome in my thoughts. I never thought, *You know what? This is all going to work out.*

> **Try reframing, "This will never work out" to "You know what? This is all going to work out."**
> **#TheMoreYouNoa**

While I was spending all of this time fixated on the past or worrying about the future, not only was I negatively obsessing over things that I couldn't change or control, but I was also squandering my life by neglecting to actually **live it**. I was never in the present. I was always missing the moment because I was constantly approaching my life from a place of fear.

The key to living freely and appreciating your life is to understand that the only time that matters—the only time that is actually *real*—is NOW. Everything else only exists in your mind and is essentially a figment of your imagination. So why live there? Why not live here, today, in this moment, in this very second?

How do you stop yourself from looking backward and forward rather than appreciating the present moment?

I want to share with you a pivotal story from my life that helped me to understand the importance of this concept better. It starts with what I call *the new notebook theory.*

When I was in high school, I used to get these 3-ring binders that had these blue denim covers. At the start of the school year, I would get one of these binders and organize my loose-leaf paper into different sections. I'd use colored dividers and neatly label them by subject matter—red for English, orange for Math, yellow for History, green for Science, and so on. In the front, I'd attach a little zip pouch stocked with pens, pencils, erasers, and a little pencil sharpener.

I would pack everything up, and I would be like, *Ok, I'm ready for the first day of school.* Everything was neat and perfect. But very quickly—every year, without fail—the binder became a complete disheveled mess. There were scribbles all over the front cover; the pages were scattered and disorganized; and I hadn't taken any notes. On the contrary, instead of taking notes, I always just wound up using the loose-leaf paper to roll joints.

This behavior was a consistent pattern in my life. This binder was just a metaphor for how I approached everything. I would start something with the best of intentions, but soon it would just be a mess. My binder, my job, my relationship, and every other aspect of my life. I meant well and wanted success, but I just couldn't get out of my own damn way. Just like the notebook, everything would quickly fall apart.

So, by 1988 I was living in Manchester, Connecticut. I had met a girl in a rehab in Mississippi, and nine weeks later, we were married. She already had two kids from a previous relationship. I was 24 years old.

I was barely sober at this point, but I had managed to get myself a decent job. I wore a suit every day, drove a nice car—you know, the American dream. I was helping my wife take care of her two children, who I really loved. I felt like I was finally on a solid path, even though I was sneaking drugs and alcohol whenever I could.

Unfortunately, the marriage—as promising as it was, born in a rehab facility—lasted only 11 months. When we separated, I moved out of our house and into an apartment nearby. On my first night in my new apartment, I remember just sitting with this overwhelming feeling of shame. I was such a fuck-up. No one else in my family had ever been divorced. But, of course, here I was. Here I was again, having had tried and failed—I tried to build a life with someone; I tried to help her parent her children; I tried to help support them with a good job; I tried to have a normal life. And, again—just like the notebook—it all fell apart.

And in that moment—having lost it all and finding myself alone once again—I just decided I had finally had enough. I was tired. I was done creating chaos and wreaking havoc all around me. And for the first time in almost eight years of bouncing around rehabs, hitting rock bottom again and again, and indulging in destructive behavior, I said to myself, *Not anymore. This is done. Tonight, I'm actually going to take this moment and do something positive with it.*

So that night, I walked into an AA meeting voluntarily for the first time in my life. I joined the meeting well after it started and left well before it ended. I could barely stand it. But I went.

Then the next night, because I was curious to see what would happen if I decided that things could actually work out for me, I went back again. I arrived a little less late and left a little less early. And then the next day, I did the same thing. And the next day. After a week or so, I started showing up early and staying well past the end of the meeting.

Once I was comfortable enough, I began sharing at meetings. My ego was huge in these early days of sobriety—I thought I deserved a medal for everything I said. The reality was, I had been in enough rehabs and was a skilled enough bullshitter and hustler that I was convinced I could con anyone into thinking that I had my shit together when I absolutely did not.

So, at this one particular meeting, I shared about how tough my day was—*I was at the mall, and I felt like drinking, but I powered through it,* blah, blah, blah. I gave this big, self-aggrandizing speech about how strong and incredible I was for managing not to drink when confronted with the urge. A big old pat on the back for me.

This guy sitting in front of me turned around to look at me. He looked like Bluto from Popeye. He had a big bushy beard, black hair, and tattoos on both forearms. "You're an alcoholic," he said matter-of-factly. "That's what you do—you want to drink. We all want to drink. That's our thing." And then he turned back around.

I was furious. *Who does this guy think he is? He was talking to ME like this? Does he know who I am? He's fucking with the wrong dude.*

During a break in the meeting, we were both standing outside smoking cigarettes. Bluto was standing up the block, about 20 feet away from me. Suddenly I heard him call, "Hey!"

I looked up, and this motherfucker flicked his cigarette butt into the gutter, pointed at me, and started walking towards me. He was tall—probably around 6'3 and built like a mountain man. His jaw was locked, and his expression was menacing.

As he closed the distance between us, I took off my watch and rings and shoved them into my pockets to ready myself for a fight. I shifted my weight to my back foot and clenched my fist.

But as he approached, he just introduced himself, "I'm Johnny Kaye," and then wrapped his arms around me and pulled me into the warmest bear hug I had ever experienced. All of the tension in my body melted away, and I just surrendered and allowed myself to feel present in the moment as I hugged him back.

Given my attitude, I probably needed the shit kicked out of me. But what Johnny knew I needed more was to be loved, cared for, and understood.

"I got you, bro. It's going to be okay," I remember him saying.

In that moment, all of my anxiety about my past, all of my fear about the future, all of my ego, just slipped away, and I was fully present in the experience. And to this day, over 30 years later, I can still remember every single second of that hug, and it reminds me of the power and importance of appreciating the now.

Over the next year, Johnny became my mentor, father, brother, uncle, and best friend. It turned out he lived only a block away from me with his crazy family—his two amazing daughters, his loud wife, and his Cuban father-in-law. I would walk up the block every morning to go have breakfast with all of them; being there just felt like home.

Johnny showed me how to make my fucking bed and how to clean myself up. He showed me what AA really was and how important it would be for me, and what the 12 steps were, and how to really commit to those learnings and way of life. He showed me how to be a man and how to not drink and how to be okay not drinking and doing lines and that I wasn't a complete fucking waste of time, and my life didn't have to end in misery and poverty and destruction. I didn't have to kill myself, and I could live and be happy like those people I watched that morning from my car—the ones who were happy and living in color. I could live in color, too.

So that moment—that hug—introduced me to one of the most influential people in my life and opened the door to one of the most significant times in my personal growth.

Being present in my life gives me peace of mind, so I'm constantly challenging myself to work on it. Whenever I'm in a bad place emotionally, I focus on the present moment—the now—and like Bluto's hug, it helps me release my anger, anxiety, and fear.

When I'm able to say to myself, *Right now, I'm okay. Right now, I'm safe*, then I realize I'm actually okay. The thoughts about the things that I had done in the past, or what will become of me in the future, are just that—meaningless thoughts that are distracting me from living peacefully.

> **When you're able to say, "Right now, I'm okay. Right now, I'm safe," then you realize you're actually okay. You realize that in this moment, everything is perfect, and you are allowed to experience the now in its purest form and take comfort in that. #TheMoreYouNoa**

Life is a series of moments, and those moments are made up of the choices we make. Ask yourself, "Do I choose love, or do I choose fear?" There are 86,400 seconds in each day. In each one of those seconds, you are making a choice to love or to fear; to live in the present, or to live in the past or the future. The goal is to appreciate each moment as it comes and to savor it while it's here.

Suggested Technique: Clap Your Hands

Here's a technique for training your brain to focus on the now: **clap your hands.** Do it now. Put down this book and just clap your hands once. Hear that sound. Recognize the fact that as soon as you hear that sound, the moment is gone. Now clap your hands again. Hear that sound. Now that moment is gone. Every time you focus on clapping your hands, you're bringing your attention to the now, and the now is all that's real. There's no past or future, just right here, right now. Life passes one single moment at a time, and the more conscious you are of that, the lighter your burden will feel.

Suggested Technique: Feel Your Feet

There's an old Buddhist meditation technique that requires you **to feel your feet.** I want you to sit down somewhere comfortable and feel the connection between the earth and you. As you focus on that connection, you will feel a sense of calm take over.

Just feel your feet. Again, you can post this statement wherever you need to see it as a daily reminder, like by your computer at work. You can write it on your hand. Put a regular notification on your phone. In any moment, if you're feeling anxious, just feel your feet. Ground yourself in the moment.

It's the only thing that's real, and you'll feel a sense of release.

Suggested Technique: Meditation

Meditation is also a critical skill to help you live in the present moment. It's certainly one of the most useful skills I've learned to help me get through my challenges, and yet I find that it eludes so many people because they just don't understand it. I'm going to guess that anyone reading this book, in the not-so-distant past, has taken some sort of medication—even if it's as simple as Tylenol or Advil for a headache. Some of us take more significant prescription drugs, but even the oldest among them is no more than 100 years old.

On the other hand, meditation is a practice with proven healing properties and has been around for 7,000 years. People have been using meditation to change their lives and improve their mental, spiritual, and even physical conditions for many millennia. So, if you're willing to take a pill manufactured in a lab 60 years ago to take away your headache, why wouldn't you be willing to try a mental discipline that has been tested and proven effective at healing for far longer?

People who resist the practice of meditation often say, "I can't sit for that long" or "I can't get my brain to quiet." Can you sit still for 10 seconds? Can you at least *try* to quiet your mind for 10 seconds? You can do anything for 10 seconds.

As a kid, I was hyperactive—which they now call ADHD—and I had to run and play until I was utterly exhausted to the point where I could barely eat dinner with my eyes open before passing out at the table. I had to wear myself down so I could relax.

Today, doctors give kids with ADD or ADHD stimulants to help them focus. I personally didn't need a stimulant—the last thing I needed was more energy. What I needed was for something to calm me down and bring my body and mind into its intended state of peace. This is how I focus and relax my mind today.

I recommend getting a meditation app, like **Headspace**, which is perfect for beginners. But there are a ton of them out there, so I recommend doing a bit of research and finding one that is the right fit for you personally.

Once you find a meditation app you like, make it part of your daily ritual, just as I discussed earlier with respect to making a gratitude list. So, for example, in the morning after I wake up, I have my coffee, and I write my gratitude list. Just after that, I'll do 10-20 minutes of guided meditation. You don't need to start with 10 minutes—just do 5 minutes, if you'd prefer. Just listen. Be a student. Be open to this practice working for you, and don't give up too quickly—it takes time for meditation to click.

Even though I had tried meditation many times and gone to events where they had meditation sections, and I'd meditated at the end of yoga classes, it took me a very long time to actually learn how to meditate. I knew how to be still, but my mind ran all over the place while I was allegedly meditating. And for those of us who are experiencing deep and profound emotional pain, that pain is an indication that your brain is running wild, just like a wild horse. When trying to capture a wild horse, you have to get a rope around it, and that's exactly what meditation did for me. It helped me rein in my brain.

It takes a long time after getting a rope around a horse's neck before you can actually ride that horse. There are a lot of steps in between. You have to calm the horse down, relax it, and get it used to you. Similarly, with meditation, calming is key. It takes a while to calm the brain down to a point where meditation can start sinking in a little bit deeper, and when it does, it's a magical experience.

I've been meditating for many years now, in many different ways and using many different practices, and the utility of the practice and the depths of healing it offers never ceases to amaze me.

In the summer of the year before I wrote this book, I got into a big fight with my girlfriend. She was hurt and angry with me, and I was convinced this was the end of the relationship. I left to spend time at a friend's house, and he had another guest there—Moni—who had just come back from her third silent meditation retreat in India. I was so on edge, and all of my nerves were firing. I hadn't had a cigarette in almost a year but broke down and went to the store to buy a pack and immediately started chain-smoking to try to calm myself down.

Moni looked at me, told me to put the cigarettes away, and instructed me to lie in the grass in my friend's backyard. "I'm going to lead you through a guided meditation," she said.

"No, that's not necessary," I resisted. At this point, I had been meditating on my own for many years, but my mind was racing all over the place, and my nerves were so wracked that I couldn't see how even meditation could help me.

"Let's just try it," she urged.

As I lay in the grass, Moni gently guided me through a thirty-minute meditation session. At the end of it, I sat up, opened my eyes, and felt an overwhelming sense of calm. My anxiety felt manageable. I got up and threw my cigarettes in the garbage.

It's not what's going on around us or specific events that cause the chaos in our lives; it's how we process those events that creates the havoc. Meditation gives you the opportunity to pull back, remove yourself from the events, undo your emotional attachment to the events, and look at things from a more objective perspective in the current moment.

So, I meditate to alleviate confusion, discontent, anger, and resentment and to ground myself in the now. In doing so, I quiet my mind, stop escaping into the past and panicking about the future, and can live calmly and peacefully.

CHAPTER FOUR

STOP THINKING THOUGHTS THAT SCARE YOU

∞

But how many corners do I have to turn? How many times do I have to learn? All the love I have is in my mind.

--The Verve, Lucky Man

Many years ago, I had a friend and mentor named Hank. Hank was an interesting character. I met him at an AA meeting, but he quickly became much more than just some guy I met at a meeting. I had a great relationship with Hank and respected him a lot. I used to call him for advice on pretty much everything.

I remember one time I called him to tell him about some problem I was having with a girl, something that seemed super significant to me at the time. I delivered this long monologue about what was going on, and he said, "Stop thinking thoughts that scare you," and hung up the phone.

I thought, *Okay, he's an old man, he probably made a mistake.*

So, I called him back. "Hank, you hung me. Let me tell you about what happened. Blah, blah, blah…."

And, again, he goes, "Stop thinking thoughts that scare you," and hung up the phone.

I did this three or four times. I called him back and started to speak, and he just continued to hang up on me after saying, "Stop thinking thoughts that scare you."

And then I finally realized: *Hold on a second. Maybe he's trying to teach me something.* Giving it some thought, I started to understand what he was trying to say. Nearly every thought I had was scary, and I had to stop thinking about things from a place of fear.

I talked earlier about when we look to the past, we have regrets, and when we live in the future, we worry and have anxiety.

> **When I'm looking back or forward, I'm missing the sacred presence of my life. I'm not available for myself or the people around me. I'm in a state of self-obsession. All I'm thinking about is me. #TheMoreYouNoa**

So, here's the deal. When I'm like that, I'm thinking about me, how horrible I am, and how awful things are going to befall me. That is not a recipe for success. That's delusional thinking. It's ridiculous thinking. It's not based on truth. It's just me creating these stories in my mind about how horrible everything's going to work out. It's craziness because I'm actually creating the very obstacle that will prevent things from working out well!

So, I really began to take that simple phrase that Hank gave me—**stop thinking thoughts that scare you**—and started to use it as a tool of affirmation. Hence, when I find myself in that fearful state of mind, I pause and say to myself, *Noa, stop thinking thoughts that scare you.* I repeat it as many times as I need until the anxiety passes. Fear causes a lot of disruption in our mind, body, and spirit. Remember, we're built like a three-legged stool: mind, body, spirit; or mind, body, and soul, as some people like to say. If one of the legs of the stool is really short, you cannot sit down comfortably—the stool is useless. All of our mind, body, and spirit must be aligned for us to be well.

> **"Stop thinking thoughts that scare you"** is an affirmation that allows your mind and spirit to calm, and helps your breath move through your lungs more freely, which allows your body to relax."
> #TheMoreYouNoa

Fear will pop up from time to time, but now you have a tool to help you manage it and train yourself to understand that the fear is not real. To complete the focus, say: *Who I am in this moment is real. This is my truth. Not the scary thoughts I have about myself. Not the miserable thoughts I have about who I am.*

Six months after I got divorced, I was still having a pretty hard time. As I mentioned earlier, my ex-wife had two kids from a previous relationship, so I inherited a six-year-old step-daughter and a four-year-old stepson, and I really, really loved them. Being separated from them was probably the most difficult part of the divorce.

About a week after we separated, I went back to our house to pick up some things. When I arrived, my stepson, who was just parroting his mother's words, looked at me and said, "We don't love you anymore." My stepdaughter just stood there silently, with tears streaming down her face.

This was like a knife in my heart.

I said goodbye, told them I loved them and that I was sorry to have to leave them, but that was what their mom thought was best.

Months later, I was driving around the boondocks of Connecticut, selling advertising for a local newspaper. This was before cell phones, so I pulled over at a payphone on the side of the road to call my parents. My father answered.

Now, my father is a loving, kind person, but he's never been big on expressing his feelings. He speaks with his actions, less with words. Quite often, even to this day, I will end our conversation with, "Alright, I love you, Dad." And he'll say, "Okay, bye." It's not that he doesn't love me. I know he does. This is just his personality.

My father just happened to be the person to pick up the phone that day. He asked how I was doing.

I explained, "You know, Dad, I'm not doing well. I'm not doing well at all. I'm having a really tough time."

I didn't ordinarily open up to him, but at this point, I

was starting to try change my life for the better and applying some of the tools that I had been learning during the course of my recovery. Being honest and truthful about how I felt when someone asked me how I was doing became a regular practice and valuable tool.

"What's going on?" he asked.

"I really miss the kids," I said. "I miss seeing them and holding them and loving on them."

My father said something then that has remained with me to this day. He said, "Noa, I don't know many truths, but I do know this: every rainstorm in the entire history of the world has been followed by a sunny day."

That really hit me. And it has hit a ton of people who I've shared it with the same way because it's just a simple truth. It's just a practical thought that helps you contextualize your feelings. You can wrap your mind around this comforting truth and use it as a tool to give you hope and assurance that anything you're going through right now is only temporary. Things will get better.

> **You have successfully lived through every single struggle that you've ever endured in your life. You've overcome every single challenge in your life so far, and you're still here reading this book. Just by reading this book, you're taking action and making progress towards improving your life. And as long as you're alive, you have the power to change and grow for the better. #themoreyounoa**

Our mind is where it all starts. Once I started reducing my fear-based thinking, I had a greater capacity to love. I'm left with this void into which love just flows. I don't even have to be intentionally loving. When you clear fear and feel more relaxed, you feel more at ease with everything that's going on in your life. From that place, you naturally become a more kind and loving person who is more aware of the beautiful effect you can have on the world and, in return, the beautiful effect the world can have on you.

You want more love in your life? Grow it. Focus on love. Stop thinking thoughts that scare you, and then you can start to have loving thoughts instead. You can just replace them. You can switch the narrative. Instead of thinking: *What if it doesn't work out?* Change your perspective and think: *What if everything works out perfectly?*

What if you *do* get that job? What if you *do* get that raise, that promotion, that girl, or that guy you like? Whatever the thing is that you're hoping for—what if you *do* get it? Or what if you don't? And what if you don't get it, but you get something even better than you could have imagined? Because usually, that's exactly what happens. What you think you want may not work out, but that's only because there's something better waiting for you beyond what you dreamed of.

Suggested Technique: List 10 Things You Hope Will Happen

If you're reading this book right now and following through with the tools that I've given you, I want you to stop and **write down ten things** you hope will happen in the next year. Then, I want you to take that piece of paper and put it away in a place where you won't look at it for a year.

Set a calendar notification for one year from now that says, "Go back and look at the list," and I guarantee you, you will have shortchanged yourself. You have no idea how big your life can get. You just can't imagine it, and love grows exponentially. It grows so much faster than fear. Once you take the fear away and you start to act in love, it just expands. It overpowers everything. It creates this incredible abundance.

CHAPTER FIVE

YOU ARE NOT A WATER SPILLER

∽

Wake now, discover that you are the song that the morning brings. But the heart has its seasons, its evenings, and songs of its own.

--Grateful Dead, Eyes of the World

Imagine something for a moment. I want you to visualize that you get to the end of this book, and your life has changed a bit—you're taking some positive action and feeling some love pouring into your life. You come to meet me to talk about your progress. We're sitting at opposite sides of a table, and I have a bottle of water next to me. Because I use my hands a lot when I talk, I knock over the bottle and spill water all over the table. I run to the bathroom to get some paper towels, and we mop it up before continuing our talk.

The next day, you meet a friend and tell her about your conversation with me. Maybe you describe what I look like, what I do for a living, my sense of humor, or how I made you feel. But would you say, "Hey, I met Noa last night. He's a water spiller."? No, of course not. You wouldn't have even thought about describing me that way.

And yet, it's easy for us to slip into this mindset where we define ourselves based on things we've done in the past or things that have happened to us. This is because we become so hyper-focused on ourselves and our own issues that we start to think that we *are* those issues.

I myself have post-traumatic stress disorder as a result of witnessing extreme violence and death early in my life. If I don't treat the PTSD, I wake up in the middle of the night with night terrors along with a whole host of other issues. While I have to manage around this, I don't equate who I am in this world with the fact that I have PTSD. My PTSD doesn't form the basis of my identity. I don't walk up to people and introduce myself as 'Noa with PTSD.'

Nobody is what has happened to them. Not in one second, one minute, one moment, six months, or one year. Nobody is defined by an action they've taken, an event they've lived through, or by something that was done to them. Experiences don't define who you are. They're just things that have happened and are now over and in the past. Shit happens. It happens to everyone. Every single person on this planet has had shit happen to them. Every person you know. Every person on the street. Everyone shares in some way, shape, or form some amount of or some version of the pain that you've felt in your life.

The truth is, you're not as unique as you think you are. We all experience love and joy, and we all experience loss and pain. We all suffer from some degree of insecurity, and we all have anxieties and fears. All human beings feel the same set of emotions, just perhaps to different extents based on different events and life circumstances. That doesn't mean that you're not wonderful and special, but when we absorb and think about our individual experiences as being so incredibly unique, we create separation and a sense of isolation that only further aggravates our problems.

Man, this terrible thing happened to me. No one could ever understand what this feels like. You'll never get me because you never experienced anything like this. This is the kind of self-focused thinking that leads you to define yourself by your pain, when in reality, your pain and the experiences that created that pain have nothing to do with who you actually are.

We all know various gradients of pain within the context of our own individualized experiences. Of course, some people have had truly horrific things happen to them—far worse than anything I've ever experienced. But there are also some people who have had terrible things happen to them which, within the context of their life, may feel magnified and huge, but when compared to the experiences of others, may actually seem pretty insignificant.

Imagine this: You're getting ready to walk into a room filled with 100 people. Before anyone enters the room, they're given a piece of cardboard and a marker and asked to write down a list of their problems. Then they're given a piece of string to fasten to the cardboard and told to hang the list of problems around their neck. When you enter the room, you begin greeting people and reading their lists.

After making your rounds, you realize you wouldn't want any of these people's problems. In fact, you would likely take your problems over any of these other problems you're seeing.

Because everyone thinks their problems are the worst until they step outside of themselves and see that everyone has their own set of issues that they're struggling with. That's just life.

Throughout my life, I've worked with celebrities, rock stars, and athletes. I've also worked with ordinary guys who just got out of prison and are trying to get their lives back on track. And, really, the feelings are all the same. The pain is just as real and can be just as overwhelming, regardless of your station in life.

Don't be fooled—money and access to opportunity don't mitigate how people feel pain. Just because someone has money doesn't mean they don't feel pain as deeply as the rest of us. We sort of assume, *Well, they're a celebrity—they've got all this money and fame, so everything must be better for them.* But it's not. Celebrities and people with access to cash hit rock bottom just as hard as ordinary people do. Money may make your life easier in certain ways, but it doesn't protect against trauma, and it doesn't cure emotional pain. Again, life events are filtered through the genetic code of human consciousness, and therefore what we feel just isn't as varied as you think.

Once I realized that my experiences did not define me, I was able to get out from under my pain rather than allow it to make me feel stuck. I've spilled a lot of water, but I'm not a water spiller. I've done a lot of shitty things, but I'm not a shitty person. Who I am today is who I am today. That's just the truth.

When you feel yourself fixating on something you've done or something that's happened to you in the past, pause and ask yourself: *So, what?* I use this as a tool to check myself so that I don't allow the experience or pain to overwhelm me and form an obstacle to my moving forward in positivity and living freely.

You lost your job? *So, what?*

Your girlfriend broke up with you? *So, what?*

This is not a flip—"it doesn't matter"—rhetorical question. It's rather intended as a tool to help you shift your focus from the negative thing that happened, which you can't control, to what your reaction will be, which you can control. So, something not awesome happened to you. Nothing will come from fixating on it. Fixating on it won't undo the event. But you can focus on how to move on from here. You can focus on the next best action you will take. What's the next step?

So, what?* means *Okay, well that happened, so what am I going to do next?

You can do this in relation to anything you're feeling upset about—any occurrence in your life that in the moment feels so tragic and desperate. Pause and ask yourself: *So, what am I going to do next? So, what? It happened, now let's move forward.*

For example: I'm an alcoholic. *So, what?* She broke my heart. *So, what?* I can never seem to lose weight. *So, what?*

What are you going to do about your drinking if you're an alcoholic?

How are you going to keep going and meet someone else if she broke up with you?

If you want to lose weight, what are you willing to change in your diet and exercise regime to make that happen?

> **So, what?** demands that you stop focusing on the problem and get to the solution. It's the only way to operate. When you're confronted with a problem, you're either living in the problem or acting in the solution. #TheMoreYouNoa

Johnny Kaye once gave me a great piece of advice, which I often turn to when I'm feeling overwhelmed by something that's happened—when I'm feeling stuck. I recently passed this advice on to a friend of mine, Dee, who had broken up with her partner of thirteen years, and I want to share it with you here because I've found it to be an incredibly useful tool when trying to let go of something.

Dee was suffering from a deep sense of loss following this breakup. She and her partner shared a life together and raised Dee's children together, and when their relationship ended, Dee was struggling to move past the pain.

Here's the tool Johnny shared with me, which I passed on to Dee. I call it **Drop the Rock**:

I want you to imagine yourself on a boat in the Caribbean Sea. It's a beautiful day. The sun is shining; blue skies stretch as far as your eyes can see; and there's a tropical breeze gently moving the boat along the water. You are surrounded by friends and family, and everyone is laughing and frolicking and having a great time.

At the bottom of the boat, beneath the deck, is a sack of gold rocks that you're transporting to an island.

Now the boat suddenly hits a reef and springs a leak. Water is flowing into the vessel, and the boat starts to go down, sinking into the ocean.

Everyone around you immediately jumps off the boat. Just about 100 yards away, and not a far swim, is a beautiful paradise island that has everything you need to survive. It has a fresh-water river running through it. It has animals running around it. It has all sorts of fruit trees growing on it.

Everyone is swimming towards the island, but you hesitate because you know there's something precious beneath the deck. You run downstairs and grab a big, heavy rock of gold and carry it up with you. You figure you're strong enough, so you jump into the water carrying this heavy gold rock and start swimming towards the island.

Everyone starts screaming at you from up ahead, "Drop the rock! Drop the rock!"

But you're like, "No, I'm good. I've got this."

But then the water starts rising up to your chin, and you're having a harder time swimming. You hear, "Drop the rock! Drop the rock!"

But you're still swimming, and you're thinking: "I've got this. I'll get there with this rock of gold, and when I do, I'll have something really valuable with me." But then you tire a bit more, and the water starts rising over your nose, and now you're taking gulps of water and struggling to stay afloat.

The lesson is, whatever you're carrying that's difficult and painful to carry, all you need to do is let it go. If you don't let go of it, you'll succumb to its weight. If you let go of it, you'll swim freely.

Whenever I'm dwelling on something painful, I start repeating to myself: **Drop the rock. Drop the rock. Drop the**

rock. This reminds me to refocus my thoughts and let go of the thing that is causing me pain, which helps me move forward with my life.

Most of us went to the beach or the waterpark at some point when we were younger. If you're like me, you loved to play in the waves and got excited by how it felt when the waves lifted you up and put you back down. As an adult, I still love to swim in the ocean and feel its power against my body.

As you got older, maybe you would swim out farther or swim into rougher waters. Even though I'm stronger as an adult, the ocean is almighty, and some of its waves are much stronger than I am. Sometimes I just get flipped upside down and lose my breath. My shorts fill with sand. It's not the most pleasant experience.

Picture yourself sitting in an inner tube in the ocean and allowing it to ride the waves—just be one with the water and allow it to carry you wherever it goes. Now, if you flip the inner tube in the opposite direction and start kicking against the current, you're going to make very little progress. You're not really going to go anywhere.

And that's life.

When you allow life to happen on life's terms, not according to what you think is best—not on the plans and imaginations you have—you flow more easily. Because, first of all, you're going to underestimate just how good things can be if you just surrender to letting things happen. But, second of all, if you're resisting the current, you're not in sync with the world. You're not learning to live life on life's terms. You're not accepting things as they come—you're resisting things you can't control. Things happen. You are not defined by those things. You just have to accept them and move forward with your next best action.

No matter what amount of pain you're in, try lifting yourself up, taking some breaths, and allowing yourself to visualize floating on the ocean and using that image to just really connect with how you're living.

One day, a guy I had worked with for years called me up screaming and bitching about how he got a parking ticket. I listened to him rant and rave for about 20 minutes, and I said, "Okay, are you done now?"

"Yeah."

"Well, you've got two choices. You can be angry that you got a ticket, or you can let that go and just be glad that you have a car. Pay the ticket and move on."

That's how we switch our thinking. Stop fixating on the things that happened to you. Filter your thoughts through a grateful lens and start living in the solution to your problems. The more we do that, the stronger that muscle gets, and the more at ease we become.

When we're able to accept life on life's terms, we complain less and feel less attacked and less overwhelmed by the events that happen to us. The less we dwell on the things that happen to us, and the more we focus our attention on positive next steps, the less likely we are to define ourselves based on our painful experiences.

CHAPTER SIX

WHEN YOU COMPARE, YOU LOSE

∾

'Cause love's such an old-fashioned word. And love
dares you to care for the people on the edge of the night,
and love dares you to change our way of caring about
ourselves.

--Under Pressure, Queen & David Bowie

Man, I spent so many years comparing myself to other people mentally, physically, socially, and financially. I was constantly telling myself I was lesser than everyone around me. Everyone had a better life. Everyone was smarter, better looking, had the wife, had the kids, the nice house, the great vacations. This was toxic thinking. By casting people in this 'better than me' role, I was automatically characterizing myself as the relative loser. When I stopped comparing myself to other people, I instantly felt better.

In this era that is so dominated by social media, where people can curate your perception of their lives, and where reality television makes ordinary people celebrities based on their wealth and excess, we can so easily get caught up in confusing the appearance of things for what is real and for what matters.

It's actually amazing how much our societal value system has changed over the last few decades. The American dream used to look like getting a good job, buying a nice car, moving to the suburbs, having a couple of kids, and being able to afford to send them to college. Now, instead of a nicely manicured lawn and a white picket fence, everyone wants to be famous. And fame is more accessible now than ever—either by becoming a social media influencer or reality TV star—you don't need any special talent or skill to become a celebrity in today's world. The problem is that people believe that fame will bring riches, and riches equal success, and success makes you feel good about yourself. But that's just wrong.

Here's the truth: feeling better about yourself has nothing to do with fame or fortune or what kind of handbag you carry, or what kind of car you drive. Feeling better about yourself is an *inside job.* It's not an outside job. Instead of focusing on what your life looks like to other people, you have to focus on your emotional and spiritual condition in order to feel good about yourself.

Comparing yourself to others creates this false sense of longing by tricking you into believing that you want things another person has just because you don't have them.

This recently happened to me when I was scrolling through Instagram. Some people I know were vacationing in Mykonos, and they were constantly posting pictures of the scenery, their boat, their food, their drinks, their parties. All of the pictures were bronze skin against an azure blue and white background, and everything looked perfect and beautiful. The group was partying in the clubs until 6 am, eating ecstasy and dancing to EDM music through the sunrise. As I sat in my bed in Brooklyn scrolling through their photos, I kept thinking to myself, *Man, I want to be in Mykonos. Why aren't I in Mykonos?*

When I was comparing myself to these people, I was automatically thinking that they had it so much better than I did. I was stuck in my studio apartment in New York City while these people were partying it up on a yacht in the Mediterranean.

But before I spiraled too far down this dangerous path, I paused and realized the insanity of what I was thinking. For starters, I don't like any of those people—they're idiots. Two, I don't do drugs. Why would I want to be in a place where everyone's doing drugs? Three, I don't like staying up late – I go to bed by 10 pm. Lastly, I fucking hate EDM music.

My comparative mind thought, *I should be in Mykonos*, but my rational mind understood that I actually didn't want to be in Mykonos at all and was perfectly happy exactly where I was. When I stopped comparing myself to these people, I realized I was being completely insane.

When we compare, we lose. When we compare ourselves to others and judge our lives by the amount of abundance of someone else's life, we lose track of the abundance in our own lives, and then we lose.

A big piece of how to manage our tendency to compare ourselves to others is by being thoughtful about who we surround ourselves with. Remember, we are the company we keep. So, if the people around you are really judgmental, jealous, mad, angry, mean, or negative, get the fuck away and find new people. If the people around you value stupid, unimportant shit, find new people. Find people who lift you up. Find people who are positive and who bring you joy. Find people who are real. #TheMoreYouNoa

Always look for opportunities to find like-minded people. You can take a class that interests you or join a club with people whose values and intentions are aligned with yours. Do you like collecting stamps? Join a stamp-collecting society. I don't even know if anybody collects stamps anymore. They used to when I was younger. Learn some pottery. Learn woodworking. There are a million things out there in the world, and the beauty is that we don't have to wander aimlessly as we did previously. Thanks to the Internet, you can google how to do things and how to find people with the same interests as you.

You know, we are absolutely the worst judges of ourselves, and no one sees us in the negative light in which we see ourselves. In my mind only, I am fat, old, broken, lost, I will never have a child, I will never get married, it's too late for me to become successful, and so on. This is all bullshit. It's all just fear-based thinking. The truth is that I have an amazing life filled with people who love me. My future has not yet been written. Through years of work, these thoughts barely creep into my mind today. But when they do, I extinguish them with the truth.

It's like going to the gym. Everyone's afraid of joining a gym because they think they're overweight or not fit, and everyone else is going to look at them. Let me tell you something—I work in the fitness industry, and nobody is looking at anybody who is working out around them because everyone is just starring in the mirror and judging themselves. People are either ego-driven, thinking, *Wow, look at how great I look*, or ego-smashed, thinking, *Wow, look at how terrible I look*.

You have to try to silence those critical voices and understand that only you are focused on yourself. Don't let the lies you tell yourself block you from accomplishing your goals.

How do you silence that critical voice in your head? How do you extinguish the lies you tell yourself with the truth? For starters, I revert to my gratitude list. Don't count other people's blessings—count your own. That's the purpose of your gratitude list. And, next, I stop myself from comparing myself to others. *I'm too old. I'm too fat. I want hair. I don't have hair. I have hair in places I don't want it.* All of these ridiculous things that we fixate on as 'bad' or 'lesser' cause us to feel shame, sadness, and depression when we need to instead be lifting ourselves up.

I want you to close your eyes and picture yourself as a young child, happy and free, running in a park. Then, put yourself there in the park in your current adult state next to that child. I want you to say all those things that you think about yourself to that child. I know when I try to do that, I can't say to my younger self, "You're fat. You're stupid. You're dumb. You're ugly. You're weird," because I know it's not true, and it's hurtful, damaging, and painful. But yet, we do it to ourselves all the time.

Don't look at somebody else's life and think that just because they're thinner, have more hair, a smaller nose, a nicer car, or a bigger house, that they're happier. It's bullshit. It's a lie. And it's all relative. You know, you're still a child. I'm 57 years old. If I met somebody who was 100 years old, they would look at me like I was a child! I try to allow myself to be childlike and play. And I try to give myself freedom from comparison, which only begets feelings of negativity and fear, so I can live in contentment and peace.

CHAPTER SEVEN

PLAY NICELY WITH THE OTHER KIDS

⌒

We're all just taller children.

--Elizabeth & the Catapult, Taller Children

Think back to when you were in grade school, and the teachers would tell you to play nicely with the other kids in the yard.

A few years ago, I discovered this song by Elizabeth & the Catapult called, 'Taller Children.' One of the lyrics is: "We're all just taller children." This struck me because it's just the truth.

> **Just because we grow in physical stature and gain knowledge through learning and accumulating experiences doesn't mean we're not still children at heart. You were born perfect and loving. At your core, you still are. #TheMoreYouNoa**

As an adult, you're just a taller version of yourself—your essence hasn't changed. The only reason that you are in emotional pain is that your mind is not in sync with your truth. The basic truth for everyone reading this is that you are a wonderful human being who was born loving and peaceful. That peacefulness is still inside of you, and you have the power to access it if you recalibrate your thinking.

Just like the schoolyard, life is a playground. The same set of rules applies. Don't bully anyone. Don't pick on anyone. Be nice to people. Stick up for people that are being picked on by others. Get between them and the bully. Stand with them. Galvanize other people to stand with them. And apply those rules to yourself just the same. Don't bully yourself. Don't pick on yourself. Be nice to yourself. Think kind thoughts about yourself.

It's important to understand that **feelings are not facts**. How you feel about something doesn't make it true. The voice in your head that attaches meaning and creates stories around the things we experience is your ego talking. Your ego's perspective is not the objective truth.

You might think, *Well, I feel like this may not work out*, but that doesn't make it true, in the same way that thinking, *I feel like I'm the greatest basketball player of all time*, doesn't make it true. When we get emotionally attached to a thought, we begin to think it's true, and when the thought is negative, we're driven towards sadness.

When I was a desperate, hopeless, hope-to-die alcoholic and drug addict, I thought that state of being was my truth and that I would forever be that person. And, yet, thirty years later, I'm nothing like that person anymore. Those thoughts were just my feelings about myself in that moment in time. They weren't actual facts about who I would become.

So, it's important to try to separate yourself from your feelings and analyze them objectively. If someone says something to you that hurts your feelings, you pause and say: *Hold on a second. What am I crying about? Someone hurt my feelings. I don't like the way that feels, but it doesn't mean that what they said is true.*

You know, you're 100 times more likely to say negative shit about yourself than anyone would ever dare say to your face. People are chickens. People are scared. But I'm brave as hell when it comes to talking shit about me. I will talk shit in my head about me all the time if I don't stop myself.

In 2006, when Facebook was still a novelty, my friend Anthony faced a difficult challenge. He had been married to his wife for thirty years and had a wonderful marriage.

He came home from dinner one night, and his wife said to him, "You want to hear the craziest thing? I just found my ex-boyfriend from high school on Facebook. How funny is that?"

"Wow, that's nuts," he said, and they laughed about how crazy it was that you could reconnect with people from different times in your life through this online social network.

At the time, Anthony was living in LA and owned a lingerie company in Mexico. So, for a week every month, he would go down to Tijuana to work in the factory. A week eventually became two weeks, and then at one point, he was spending three weeks a month in Mexico.

One time, he kissed his wife goodbye as he always did and left LA for his factory in Tijuana. When he returned a few weeks later, he found his house empty. On the kitchen counter, he found a note from his wife. "I left to be with my high school boyfriend. I'm so sorry to do this to you," it read. She had left him for the guy she had reconnected with on Facebook.

About six weeks after this happened, I attended a talk that Anthony was giving in front of a group of a hundred or so people. He spoke very openly and eloquently about his wife leaving him, both with deep feeling but also an overall sense of calm and measure.

After the talk, we went to dinner. I looked at him from across the table, and he seemed so content and serene, which was simply mind-boggling to me given everything he had gone through.

"Anthony, how did you tell the story of your breakup so calmly in front of this huge group of people? How are you so gracious about what happened? What your wife did to you after all of those years together was terrible!"

He just smiled, shook his head, and said, "No, Noa. It's not terrible."

"How are you so composed?" I pressed.

He said two things in response:

"First of all, whenever you're going through anything like this, don't try to figure it out because it doesn't matter. If God, or whatever power you believe in, came down and explained exactly what happened and why, it still wouldn't matter. It wouldn't explain anything about what to do next. So, don't try and figure out the past because it doesn't help or change anything. Focus on what comes next."

"Secondly, and most importantly, you need to move forward with **childlike curiosity about the future**."

To describe 'childlike curiosity,' I like to use this example: If I put you in a car, the first question you're going to ask me is, "Where are we going?" You'd be focused on the destination. However, if I put a little kid in a car, they just look out the window and take in the world as it goes by. They're noticing: "Fire truck! Bank! Horse! Bus!" They're just excited to point out the moments as they're happening. They're not worried about where they're headed because they're just so enthralled with the journey.

Try to approach your day with that same childlike curiosity. Be that child in the back of the car, who is fully immersed in the journey. Wonder what's coming next. Anticipate the fun. Get excited by the new things you'll see and the experiences you'll have along the way. Embrace that sense of wonder. With that renewed perspective, you'll find yourself so much more engaged with and excited by your life.

The other important lesson from Anthony was to approach every situation, even the challenging ones, with kindness.

Extinguish the anger. Anger is poison. Anger does nothing good for you. Remember that kindness wins every single time. #TheMoreYouNoa

I once had a coworker, Dan, who was in charge of a rehab

facility that I worked in, in Los Angeles. I thought he was the fucking bomb. He was my boy. We got along incredibly well, and Dan was the perfect boss. He was this cool, laid back dude, all chilled out and mellow, like a good old boy from Texas, but in the best possible way. He was a hippie in the '70s and still all about peace, crystals, and drum circles, and just good shit and good vibes. He was the kind of person who made you want to go to work every day because you just wanted to be around him and feel his energy.

At one point, Dan had a misadventure which I won't get into, but it caused him to have to leave work for a while, and so his wife, Bee, took over his job.

Now, Bee wasn't anything like Dan. She was cold and sort of rude and just completely closed off. While I tried to keep an open mind about working with her, she always gave me the feeling that she didn't like me. I internalized that negative energy and took it personally, and eventually, I decided that I didn't want to work with her anymore. Instead of looking forward to going to work every day, now I dreaded it.

I remember calling my friend Gersh to complain about Bee. "She just has the worst attitude," I explained. "For whatever reason, she doesn't like me. I might have to quit my job."

Gersh was a good friend of mine who had been sober for a long time and had become my sponsor in AA. He had more years sober than I did and was a bit wiser and more evolved than I was at this point. He said to me, "Noa, congratulations. What you have before you is a tolerance test."

"Tolerance test—what is that?"

"Your job," he explained. "You want to keep your job. So,

you're going to have to figure out how to navigate this situation with Bee so that it works for you."

"How do I do that?" I asked.

"You have to kill her with kindness. You have to be so incredibly kind—like over the top, kind—that, regardless of whether she decides to like you or not, you free yourself from this anger and negativity."

Man, I did not want to do this. I had really gotten myself into a place where I did not like Bee. I was dreading having to see her, and nothing about her made me naturally feel kind towards her. But I listened to Gersh and committed to at least give it a try.

The next morning, when I saw Bee at work, I went straight over to her, and with all the emotional energy I could muster, looked her in the eye, smiled, and asked her how she was doing. "Good Morning, Bee. How are you today?"

Bee just glowered at me in response. Her expression said: *Why are you talking to me?* And without saying a word, she quickly walked away.

The next day, when I saw Bee at work, I did the same thing. Eye contact, smile, "Hey, Bee. How are you doing today?"

She again looked at me wordlessly with an expression of disgust. *Why is this guy talking to me?* Then she quickly pushed past me down the hall.

Then, the next day I did the same thing, and again the next day, and the next. Whenever I saw Bee, I would greet her with a warm smile and ask her how she was doing. And every day, she would respond silently with a look of confusion and disdain until eventually those expressions began to fade. The scowl slowly morphed into a smile, and in time, the walls broke down.

From there, Bee and I eventually became great coworkers. But aside from working well together, we shared personal stories with each other, laughed together, and cried together. We came to understand and respect each other, and soon our professional relationship evolved into a deep friendship.

What I didn't realize about Bee when we started working together was that she was going through a very challenging time in her own life, which was deeply affecting her sense of inner peace and emotional well-being. When I met her, because I was only thinking about myself and how she was making *me* feel, I didn't realize that the energy I was receiving actually had nothing to do with me. It was instead reflective of her own struggles and the pain that she was quietly battling.

Twelve years later, Bee is in a much healthier and brighter spiritual and emotional space and is an incredibly talented life coach who shares with her clients the tools she developed on her own journey of self-discovery and healing. She remains one of my dearest friends and is a touchstone for me, especially in more turbulent times when I need some good advice. I know if I need someone to call at 4 am, Bee will answer the phone. She and her husband Dan are two of my favorite people in the world and have given me so much love and care over the years. Now, that's a massive transition from where we were when we first met, and that just shows you the power of persistent acts of kindness.

A few years ago, I was watching a film about Fred Rogers, the children's television personality and host of the show

Mister Rogers' Neighborhood. At the end of the movie, I cried, which surprised me because I don't actually cry that often while watching movies, but this one really moved me. Fred Rogers was a Presbyterian minister from Pittsburg who practiced kindness in everything that he did. Using the vast reach of television as a tool, through the simplest songs and the simplest lessons, he shared his message of kindness and self-love with a congregation of millions of young viewers over the course of a thirty-year period.

When Mister Rogers started his show in 1968, I was 5 years old, and when the last episode aired in 2001, I was nearly 40 years old. But, no matter how old I was, whenever I saw him, whenever I heard him sing his songs about love and acceptance, I felt that he was speaking to the child within me who needed to hear all of these simple yet profoundly wise and essential lessons.

Take one of his most popular songs, *It's you I like:*

It's you I like

It's not the things you wear

It's not the way you do your hair –

But it's you I like

The way you are right now

The way down deep inside you

Not the things that hide you

Not your toys—they're just beside you

This is such a simple set of lyrics, but so incredibly powerful. It reminds us that we are valuable exactly as we are—not for what we look like, or the clothes we wear or the things we have, but for who we are at our core, *inside.* It may seem silly to refer back to a children's television show to remind us of this very basic, very fundamental lesson, but understanding this fact is incredibly critical to our overall sense of well-being, and somehow, as adults, we seem to lose track of this.

I do often think of Fred Rogers as an emissary of kindness, and I go back to his teachings when I need them. After watching the film about him, I went and got a tattoo on my leg that says 'WWMRD,' which stands for: *What would Mr. Rogers do?* I look at it, and it just reminds me of the kindness and empathy he exemplified and the person I aspire to be.

So, no matter where you are in this process towards self-improvement or how much relief or freedom you feel at this moment, know that every moment that you interact with the world in any way is an opportunity for kindness. Play nice with others. Go out of your way to help people and make them feel good about themselves. Be kind to yourself and be vigilant about the thoughts you will tolerate about yourself.

> When I show kindness to others and to myself, my life becomes so big, powerful, and amazing. It responds with abundance. You get out of life what you put into it. Put kindness into your thoughts and into the world, and you'll get it back many times over. #TheMoreYouNoa

CHAPTER EIGHT

INTENTION WITHOUT ACTION
IS JUST A GOOD IDEA

∞

*And all the roads we have to walk are winding. And
all the lights that lead us there are blinding.*

--Wonderwall, Oasis

Sometime around 2005, I started hearing everyone talk
about setting their intentions: *What's your intention? Set
your intention. Cultivate your intention.* Not to mention: *I want
to be more spiritually conscious. I want to become more aware. I
want to create a vision board. I want to manifest my future.*

It became this whole phenomenon and, as it goes in our
culture, this became a trend that was embedded in many of our
conversations for that moment in time. For a long time (and
even still), everyone seemed to be talking about how to set their
intentions and manifest their dreams.

Having an intention sounds very good and lofty. 'Intention' is a beautiful word in that it implies a desire to accomplish
something and maybe even become a better person. In fact,

73

having an intention is the reason you're reading this book— you intend to feel better about yourself, to feel more at ease, to live more freely. But if I give you all of these techniques to help you improve your life and you don't do anything with them, then it may have been a good idea to buy this book, but nothing actually changes by reading it.

I'm not judging you. I know real change takes some discipline and time. Sometimes, I'll have a good idea but find it challenging to actually carry it out. It's taken me 25 years to write this book. I've thought about it a lot, but until I sat at the keyboard and actually started typing, writing a book was only a good idea. The same goes for the practices I share in this book. Every single tool here is a good idea, but unless I actually follow through by taking the action to use the tools, none of them matter.

In 2002, I was very out of shape. My neighbor was dating this woman Sam, who was teaching fitness classes in LA. One day, Sam's car pulled up in front of my house while I was pulling out of my driveway. She was blonde and tan and fit and wearing workout clothes, so I could tell by just looking at her that she must be a personal trainer.

I got out of my car and introduced myself. "Hey, do you think you can help me do anything about this?" I asked, pointing to my huge belly.

"Absolutely," she smiled. "That's what I do for a living."

"Great. I want you to train me. I want to get skinny. I want to feel good again," I said.

"Cool," she agreed. "Be ready at 8 am tomorrow morning. I'll pick you up here. Wear shorts and a t-shirt and some hiking shoes."

I'm always early, so at 7:30 the next morning, I was already in front of my house, smoking a joint and drinking a Starbucks Mocha Frappuccino—ready to get fit.

Sam picked me up as planned, and we drove to Runyon Canyon near West Hollywood. I hadn't been there before. The trail is about a 3-mile loop with beautiful sweeping views of LA and is a nice hike for a fairly healthy person. It's steep, and it'll challenge you, and you'll sweat, but it's not impossible. It can be accomplished by most in about 35-40 minutes.

One side of the trail is considerably more challenging than the other, so we took the easy route on that first day. It took me about 2.5 hours to complete because I was so out of shape. At this point in my life, I was hugely overweight and had been smoking about 3-4 packs of cigarettes a day. I had to constantly tell Sam to 'stop' on the trail just so I could catch my breath. Even hiking the easy side of the loop was leaving me gasping for air.

By the time we were halfway up the trail, I was bent over, hands on my knees, bandana just drenched in sweat. I looked like I had taken a shower in my t-shirt. I was feeling defeated but rallied myself to finish.

Noa, just take one more step. If you can take one more step, you'll be one step closer to the top. And then, after that, take another step. One step at a time. No matter how many times you have to stop, you cannot stop walking until you get to the top.

And I did just that. I kept putting one foot in front of the other, and despite the pain and the struggle, I eventually made it to the top of the climb.

I got to tell you, the last 100 feet of that climb were absolutely brutal. People were just walking by at a moderate pace, and it felt like they were whizzing past me. But when I finally got to the top, gasping for air, that feeling—that righteous, overwhelming enjoyment and satisfaction from accomplishing a task I knew (or at least I thought) was impossible—was incredible.

It's with that same tenacity that I've pursued other climbs in my life—both literal and figurative—ever since.

Now, that doesn't mean that I haven't had bad times since the first Runyon Canyon hike. I lost a bunch of weight when I was training with Sam. I got skinny and bought all new clothes and felt amazing. But then I stopped training and stopped being regimented about my habits, and I gained back all of the weight and then some. I had every intention of staying fit, but when I stopped taking actions to help me realize that goal, my intention no longer mattered.

By 2012, I was working as a counselor at a rehab center in LA. After years of destructive behavior, shame, and self-doubt, I was committed now to working with others to help them overcome similar struggles. Working with and supporting people in their efforts to achieve mental and emotional well-being has always been a symbiotic process that gives me strength and stability in my own life. Being able to do this within the context of recovery was very grounding and satisfying for me.

Yet, while my counseling work was fulfilling, I suffered

from the fact that I was once again in horrible physical shape. I was 300 pounds now, eating poorly, and still smoking multiple packs of cigarettes a day. Moving was a struggle. I couldn't bend over my stomach to tie my shoes, so I could only wear slip-on sneakers.

When I went to the doctor for my annual check-up, I received a grim report.

"Well, I've got some great news for you," the doctor announced. "You're not going to feel a thing."

"Oh, am I getting a shot?" I asked.

"No, you're about to have a heart attack. It's going to probably be so massive that you'll be dead before you even hit the ground." He shook my hand and added, "Good luck. It's been great knowing you," before leaving the room.

Well, that was jarring, I thought as I sat alone in the examination room. He had been telling me for years that I had to lose weight, but I just didn't listen. It wasn't that I didn't want to lose weight, but I was reluctant to push myself and stick to a plan. After everything I'd been through—all of the near-death experiences, the suicide attempts—I really didn't want to die now because I had eaten too many Big Macs. But I also really didn't know what to do about it.

I was scared. I was scared to push my body again. I was scared that at my age, and with my diminished lung capacity, I wouldn't be able to withstand exercise. I was scared that my body would fail me and that I'd feel even more defeated and ashamed than I had already felt. And, as I've already discussed, fear can be extremely paralyzing. It's often our biggest obstacle in changing our lives and realizing our dreams.

A few weeks later, I was on my way into a shopping center on Sunset Boulevard in West Hollywood when I passed by a SoulCycle studio on its opening day. SoulCycle was a boutique spin company that had started about six years prior in New York City. I was familiar with it because Sam, the trainer who I had worked with ten years earlier, was one of the founding instructors and had since moved to New York to help build the business. Sam had become a very close friend of mine over the years, so I figured I'd stop inside and check it out.

A couple of girls greeted me from behind the front desk. I introduced myself and explained that I was a friend of Sam's, and they excitedly offered me a free class.

"Nah, it already looks pretty full," I said, as I nervously eyed all of the young, fit people in the crowd waiting to sign in.

"Come back at 3 pm," they offered. "You can ride on the house anytime. We'll save you a bike."

I hesitated at first but then decided that this must be a sign. What were the chances that I had passed by this new, trendy exercise studio that my friend had started on its opening day in LA? I was just headed to the mall to buy underwear. I didn't know that SoulCycle was opening a West Coast location, and no part of me had planned to exercise that day. It felt like the universe was trying to tell me something. So, I ran home, grabbed a t-shirt and some gym shorts, and returned to the studio for the next class.

The room was dark, but I couldn't hide the overwhelming shame and sadness I felt as I clipped into the bike. *How did I let myself get to this physical state?* I wasn't sure I would make it through the class, so I chose a bike closest to the door so the studio staff wouldn't have to carry me far to get me out of the room if I collapsed. But when the music came on, and I started pedaling to the beat, something inside of me shifted. At the very edge of my consciousness was a glimmer of hope. I hung on to that glimmer with all I had and, slowly, my confidence started to grow. Somewhere deep inside of that massively over-weight body, I was an athlete, and I knew I was going to make it through.

Few things in my life have felt as good and as satisfying as finishing that first class. Not only did it feel great to work my body after so many years, but the sense of accomplishment and awareness that I was actually capable of embarking on this path towards change was incredibly empowering.

So, I went back the next day. And then the next. And again the day after that. Soon, I was completely hooked—riding multiple times a day—at first tucked into the dark recesses of the room, and then eventually developing the confidence to ride in the front row.

SoulCycle very quickly became my sanctuary. It was a place where I could push my body and also clear my mind by letting go and just getting lost in the music. I was getting stronger and losing weight fast, and I was feeling more energized, in-creasingly confident, and happier overall. I became even more acutely aware of just how interdependent the mind and body are and how reliant each is on the health of the other.

Ninety days later, I had already lost 100 pounds. Needless to say, it blew my mind when, around the same time, the head of SoulCycle's training program suggested that I audition to become an instructor. Becoming a fitness professional was in my mind only one step away from becoming an astronaut. I was the fat guy! Could I really do this?

I was eager to try. I knew the power of SoulCycle and the impact that it had on my life. And I was confident that I would be a good instructor because teaching ran in my blood—my grandmother taught music until she was well into her 90s, and my mom still teaches yoga and dance 6 days a week at over 80 years old. If I could use SoulCycle as a platform to reach out to more people and to help them in a more holistic way to achieve mental, emotional, and physical well-being, then I would be taking my work to an entirely new level of success and personal satisfaction for me.

> It's crazy how tiny acts can change everything. I want to help you find that moment where everything changes for you because it really only takes one decision, and the direction of your life can entirely shift. #TheMoreYouNoa

A few weeks later, I was on a plane to New York City to join the instructor training program. I hadn't lived on the east coast in nearly 20 years, and when I landed at JFK, the first thing I did was call my mom and say, "Mom, I'm home. I'm home for good." I never looked back. New York is home. And I've been here ever since.

As I write this, for eight years now, I've had the privilege of teaching sold-out classes in New York City, and I have hundreds of people come to ride with me every week. I love my job.

It's given me an incredible life that I would've never dreamed of. But it wasn't my intention that got me here. It wasn't my thoughts that got me anywhere near here. **It was the actions I took that got me to this place.**

I tell this to my riders all the time: "You're here. Signing up for an exercise class is great but showing up for an exercise class is what really matters."

I always try to assure my new riders who are scared or nervous to take their first class. "If I can prove to you in one photo that you can do this, will you do it and just know that you're going to be alright?" Then I show them a picture of me from before I took my first SoulCycle class, and they gasp at the transformation.

So, if I can change everything, you can too. I was a miserable alcoholic and drug addict. Then I was sober, but I was miserably fat and unhealthy. If I can get through all of that, you can get through your troubles too.

Start by taking small steps. **Write down five things that you would like to change about your life.** Right next to each thing, write down one step you can take towards achieving that change.

It's helpful to just make a list and see it.

Things I want to Change	One Step Towards Change
1. I want to get fit.	1. Take a 20-minute strength training class online.

2. I want to write a book.	2. Set a timer and write for 10 minutes a day.
3. I want to have more energy.	3. Research energy-fueling foods online.
4. I want to learn to cook.	4. Sign up for a cooking class.
5. I want to reorganize my apartment.	5. Reorganize a small space like your bathroom.

I'm not saying there's a quick and easy fix to anything. Again, making changes in your life takes time and discipline, and seeing the results requires patience. This book isn't called '90 Days to Feel Better.' I can't offer you a pill to lose 100 pounds. Creating change takes work, but it starts with action—one small action—and then the momentum will build.

> **Remember that life doesn't change on its own. *You* have to take action to change it. #TheMoreYouNoa**

One day, before my ex-wife and I were officially divorced, I was on my way to Johnny Kaye's house to have dinner with him and his family. On my way there, I saw my ex-wife in a truck with another man in the parking lot of a 7-Eleven. I got incredibly upset, but as I walked into Johnny's house, I buried the pain and tried to hide my sadness.

"How are you doing, man?" he asked as I sat down at the table.

"I'm good, man. I'm good. I'm good."

"What's going on?" he quizzed.

"Nothing. Nothing's going on."

"You're angry," he concluded.

"No, I'm not angry."

"Yes, you are. I can tell. Noa, it's okay to be angry."

Up to that point, it seemed so foreign to me to show emotion. When I was growing up, as a guy, you were expected to be tough. You didn't cry. You didn't show suffering. You didn't admit to feeling pain, no matter how badly you were hurt. You didn't scream. You could have a broken arm, but you didn't scream. You gritted your teeth and got on with it. Rubbed some dirt in it. Kept walking.

All of these voices in my head always told me that I should act emotionless, no matter how I was feeling. Pushing everything down was all I knew.

As we continued to talk, I explained to Johnny how much I wanted things to be different and how much I wanted to alter the way things were going in my life.

He said something to me then that I'll never forget. He said to me, "**Life does not change. The only thing that changes is how you react to it**."

So, even though I'm sober and at peace and full of joy, and I have all of these tools that help me manage my thoughts and emotional well-being, I've still had shit happen. I've been fired. That's okay. I've had my heart broken. That's okay. I've had not awesome things happen to me that I couldn't control. But what I could control was how I responded to those things.

Using some of these tools, you will feel stronger. You may not knowingly put yourself directly in harm's way. But if you do experience something that doesn't feel great or is less than optimal, you will feel more at ease accepting the situation and more equipped to push through it with the knowledge that you are in control of your response and that you will be okay.

You may now be on a new path and starting to climb out of what feels like an emotional pit of despair. If you're stuck anywhere on a mountain or in a forest, you've got to find your way out. You've got to summon the willpower and strength and use the tools to find your way. And sometimes, you may stumble.

> **We all stumble. Everyone reading this book has lost their footing and fallen. But you pick yourself up. You get back up. And eventually, you walk again. #TheMoreYouNoa**

Accept that, even after you pick yourself back up, you will likely stumble again. That's part of life. Accept that. Accept that we're fallible. We are not perfect. We are trying. But no one stumbles and stays on the ground forever. You can't stumble and stay in your pain forever. You've got to get up and keep going.

I was in an Uber about eight weeks ago, and the driver and I began talking because, although I don't like to annoy the drivers, I will talk to an Uber driver if they seem friendly, as I like to meet new people.

So, my driver was from Nepal and was Sherpa and mountain guide who lead people up the Himalayas, including up Mount Everest.

I said, "Wow! Have you been to the top of Everest?"

"Oh, I've been up there many times," he said. "My whole family—my father, my grandfather, my great-grandfather—were all climbers. We climbed Mount Everest because that was what we did; that was our lives."

"Wow, you must be incredibly strong," I said.

"No. It's not the body that carries you up Everest," he explained. "It's the mind. Your mind is what carries you to the summit. I was born into this way of life, and this is my job and my work, but this is also my joy. So, I never think about my body when I'm climbing. I don't train. I feel as though my life has trained me for the mountain. My mind carries me up, especially when times are more difficult and challenging. Even if your muscles don't work, your mind will. You've got to keep a beautiful, open mind to the possibility that you can reach the summit, that you can accomplish this great task that lies ahead. And with that strength of mind, your body will follow."

Now, of course, people train their entire lives to be able to climb Everest, and many don't survive. It's not as easy for everyone to rely solely on their minds to summit the tallest mountain in the world. But his perspective was so interesting and such an important lesson to keep in mind when confronting a challenging task.

Now, I personally have nearly destroyed my life many times. But one thing I do have is persistence. People I used to work with on construction sites called me 'Bulldog' or 'Pitbull,' because I used to attack the task at hand with unwavering tenacity. I would shovel dirt until my hands bled.

Write this down, or just screenshot it. **You have the tenacity of a bulldog and the strength of a tiger.** Own that. That tenacity and strength are inside of you. No matter who you are. If you think you're not tenacious, you're wrong because, after all, you're still here. If you think you don't have strength, you're wrong; you maybe just haven't tapped into it yet.

Trust in your tenacity. Trust in your strength. Harness those powers to begin to attack your dreams. Don't just set an intention. Dreams don't just manifest themselves. Act on your intentions. Chase your dreams. Everything you need to achieve what you want is already inside of you.

CHAPTER NINE

HELPING OTHERS TO HELP YOURSELF

∽

The best way to find yourself is to lose yourself in the service of others.

--Mahatma Ghandi

Perhaps the most powerful tool I can share with you is to encourage you to be of service to others. There is not a single action you can take to improve your life that will be more effective than turning your attention outward to helping other people.

Many of the great women and men throughout history whom we revere embodied this very fundamental concept—from Mahatma Gandhi to the Dalai Lama, to Mother Theresa, to Martin Luther King, Jr., to Fred Rogers, and many, many more. What they all understood is what matters most in life is helping others. And through helping others, you create a life of fulfillment and joy and ultimately help yourself.

Every morning, I ask my protector, my universe, whatever that power and energy is in the world that looks over me, how I may be of maximum service today to my fellow human beings. I ask to be shown opportunities, and almost every single day, I'm given that privilege.

Again, this is an intention. My primary intention in my life is to help others. After taking and taking and causing so much pain in the world to myself and others, I've discovered that my way forward and the only way for me to live with a good conscience and heart is to give of myself to other people. It takes away my self-pity and my low sense of self-worth because when I'm focused on others, I'm not focusing on myself.

I always say, **the more I think about myself, the less I think of myself.** When I spend time focusing on myself, I pick myself apart and ultimately wind up feeling terrible. But when I stop focusing on myself, I feel much better, more energized, and with a greater sense of purpose.

Being of service to others doesn't mean you necessarily have to carry their grocery bags or deliver lunch. There are thousands of ways you can be helpful. You can feed the homeless. You can volunteer in a women's shelter. You can donate money to a cause you are passionate about. You can donate your professional skills on a pro bono basis. You can buy school supplies for teachers. You can join your local community board. You can pick up litter in your local park. But you can also compliment someone. You can tell your friends how much you appreciate them. You can hold the door open for someone struggling to get through.

Most of us get coffee in the morning at a local coffee shop, at least once in a while, if not all the time. How about if when you walk up to the counter, you actually acknowledge your barista for the person they are rather than just as the hand that prepares your coffee? Your barista has their own life, with its own complexities—family, friends, relationships, jobs, rent, mortgage, healthy, sick, whatever. Rather than dehumanize them, let them know you *see them*. They often wear a name tag—read it. Smile at them and then say, "Good morning, Francesca. How's your day going? Good morning, Cara. How's your day going?"

It may feel forced and unnatural at first but just try it. It takes hardly any effort. You will see their eyes light up in response to being humanized and seen. And I promise you; you will start to feel very fulfilled.

After they hand you your coffee, say, "Thank you so much for making this for me." And then you'll also feel your gratitude kick in. You can even remind yourself how grateful you are to be able to buy yourself a cup of coffee. Now you're tying gratitude and service together.

I have this thing that I love to do on the 5th day of every month. I call it 'Take 5 to Give 5.' In the morning, I put $5 in my pocket and find someone to give it away to during the day. Sometimes I give it to a homeless person. Sometimes I buy the person behind me on line at Starbucks a cup of coffee. Sometimes I give it to a co-worker to help pay for their lunch. For a whopping total of $60 a year, I find some peace knowing that I've made 12 people's days better in some small way.

And know that when you take a small act of kindness, it's like throwing a stone into a pond—there will be a ripple effect. Whoever receives your kindness is likely to pass it on. And you never know who it's going to hit. You never know how much someone really needs it. That chain reaction that you ignite can wind up making a huge difference in someone's life.

Why do we do this?

> We help others because we're building a bank of positivity, love, kindness, and gratitude, and holding that bank increases our sense of self-worth and mitigates self-pity, doubt, and pain. When you build a bank of positivity, you can draw strength from that bank. #TheMoreYouNoa

Because, like I said earlier, just because you change doesn't mean that life is going to change with you. You're going to continue to experience everything that life holds—job loss, loss of a loved one, heartbreak, broken relationships. But by building up a bank of positivity, you'll have an easier time navigating those challenges when they arise.

If I start from a place of self-pity, self-loathing, and fear, and then something shitty happens to me, I'm going to end up spiraling and feeling really terrible. But if I focus on putting love into the world; focus on kindness, gratitude, and service; if I focus on improving my mental, physical and spiritual condition by using some of the tools I've shared in this book, then I will feel far more capable of getting through the rough times.

This book is an act of service for me. In this book, I've shared some anecdotes about my life with you, and I've given you some valuable techniques that have helped me on my journey. As I said in the very beginning, if I can help even one person ease their pain, then this work has been worth it. Because that's the ultimate joy—bringing others peace and serenity and helping others on their path towards a brighter way of life.

Helping others feeds your soul, and your soul is your essence. When you feed that essence—that beautiful part of you, that perfect part of you, that child inside of you—when you wrap that child up in love, comfort, joy, and strength—then you feel good about yourself, and you spread those good feelings to others.

That's the highest form of love you can put into the world.

POSTSCRIPT

And he still gives his love; he just gives it away. The love he receives is the love that is saved. And sometimes is seen a strange spot in the sky. A human being that was given to fly,

-- Pearl Jam, Given to Fly

I'm so grateful that you took the time to read this book. I hope you found it to be a useful resource, and I hope that you find that the tools I've shared help you release some of your pain and live with greater peace. I want you to learn to love your life, as I finally learned to love mine.

I want to tell you one last story. I want you to picture of an aircraft carrier. Now, these ships are huge, some weighing up to 300,000 tons. Imagine having to turn that vessel around to go in a completely different direction. It's going to take a lot of focus and a lot of small moves to change its course against the changing tides and rolling waves.

Changing the course of your life is much the same process. If you do the work and use the tools I've shared, you will slowly find yourself making progress towards your goal. It takes time, but it's completely achievable. Like the aircraft carrier, once you get going in a new direction, you'll feel strong and powerful and in sync with the force of the current of your life.

Be patient with yourself in this process.

Be kind to yourself in this process.

Love yourself.

Made in United States
Orlando, FL
28 January 2023

29171150R00064